If I can stop one heart from breaking,
I shall not live in vain;
If I can ease one life the aching,
Or cool one pain,
Or help one fainting robin
Unto his nest again,
I shall not live in vain.

EMILY DICKINSON
'If I Can Stop One Heart from Breaking'

THE NATURE CHRONICLES PRIZE
−2−

WINNING ENTRIES

WITH AN INTRODUCTION BY
MARCHELLE FARRELL

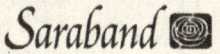

Published by Saraband
3 Clairmont Gardens,
Glasgow, G3 7LW

www.saraband.net

Copyright © Saraband 2025
Copyright in individual essays remains with the authors
Cover photograph 'Frosted bracken' © Madeleine Scott

*Published in association with
the Prudence Scott Charitable Trust*

All rights reserved. No part of this publication may be reproduced, stored in a retrieval system, or transmitted, in any form or by any means, electronic, mechanical, photocopying, recording, or otherwise, without first obtaining the written permission of the copyright owner.

ISBN: 9781916812406

Printed and bound in Great Britain by Clays Ltd, Elcograf S.p.A.

1 3 5 7 9 10 8 6 4 2

CONTENTS

MARCHELLE FARRELL: Introduction — 1

The Winning Essay
MATT SOWERBY: Hope is the Thing with Flippers — 9

The Shortlisted Essays
NIELLAH ARBOINE: Into Each Life, Some Rain Must Fall — 35

MEG BERTERA-BERWICK: The Kailyards — 47

EMMA HARDING: Wild Track — 81

DAVID HIGGINS: Minibeasts — 93

NEHA SINHA: Ibis Sea — 109

ENDNOTES — 127

THE JUDGES — 133

ACKNOWLEDGEMENTS — 137

MARCHELLE FARRELL

INTRODUCTION

In this time when multiple, interconnected crises – social, economic, physical and mental health, environmental, war – affect every aspect of our lives, what role is there for nature writing? In the pastoral, observational form which the genre is traditionally imagined to take, perhaps there is little scope beyond the soothing escapism into that sanctuary that natural spaces can provide to those who are able to access them. But even as we judges of this year's Nature Chronicles Prize escaped into the soothing setting of Windermere, near where the prize's benefactor lived, in order to consider, debate and select this year's most powerful and memorable essay submissions, we all believed that the genre has a crucial and timely role to play. It is a role we felt sure Prudence Scott herself would recognise, had she been invited to interrogate the urges that compelled her to write her own nature diaries.

The interlinked quality of the challenges of our age shines a light on our profound interdependence with the other living creatures with whom we share this precious Earth. Ultimately those

INTRODUCTION

challenges are often the result of forgetting or suppressing the knowledge that we rely on the rest of the natural world for our survival. Nature writing can remind us of who we are as a species, and of our integral role in the natural order of things. It can shift our perspective, so that we see ourselves and our place in the fabric of life more accurately. From that place of insight, it can urge us to act, and even change our behaviour, so that we might live from a place of generosity and reciprocity with the world around us, rather than from a place of exploitation and greed.

It is that sense of urgency, combined with a perspective that felt fresh and new, that led to the unanimous choice of 'Hope is the Thing with Flippers' as this year's winner. Matt Sowerby caused us all to reconsider what encountering nature in the middle of central London might mean, making us look at the too-familiar skeleton of a whale suspended in the middle of the Natural History Museum in a different light. He also brought a new and urgent activist voice that we were excited to hear. And importantly, despite sharing difficult facts about our relationship with the natural world, this piece brought us hope, that much needed quality that can keep us driving towards change against all the odds of pessimism and despair. We cannot wait to see what Matt will write next.

MARCHELLE FARRELL

Meg Bertera-Berwick's emotionally evocative piece 'The Kailyards' was another unanimous favourite of the 2023/'24 judging panel. This was nature writing that made us feel deeply. We found the way in which the writer deftly linked her attempts to grow in the uncertain ground of a rented front garden with the history of tenancy on the land and the forgotten vegetable for which the area is named to be tenderly provocative. Meg shed light on the sometimes brutal aspect of land ownership, and made us think about the fragility of our relationship with the rest of the natural world if we are unable to feel secure and grounded in a place.

From one woman growing in Scotland, we met another coming into relationship with growing in the south of England, but in a very different way. Niellah Arboine writes about moving from London to a farm in the countryside, and the tangled interrelationships between herself, the natural world around her in the city and country, and the experience of spending time in Jamaica with her grandmother in the quietly beautiful 'Into Each Life Some Rain Must Fall'. We found her perspective surprising, with a warmth and humour that helped us to look again at our feelings about some of the creatures with whom we most commonly share space – summer wasps, so much less lauded in writing than bees – and find new affection for these sometimes annoying neighbours.

INTRODUCTION

'Minibeasts' by David Higgins also brought a new perspective to everyday encounters, juxtaposing crane flies and fatherhood in an unexpected and enjoyable way. His piece also wonderfully highlighted the ambivalence inherent in our relationship with nature, demonstrating how deep awe and wonder can coexist with fear and anxiety, often within the same moment.

The fear and anxiety associated with being a woman trying to access the natural world was profoundly highlighted in Neha Sinha's beautiful piece, 'Ibis Sea'. This writing also brought us another international point of view, this time from Delhi in India. It also taught us something new by showing us the seemingly carnivorous ibis birds sipping nectar from the vivid flowers of the Semal tree in the middle of Delhi's urban wilds – imagery that evoked a collective intake of breath from the judging panel.

Grief was a common trope in the pieces that we read, but nowhere was it handled as masterfully as in Emma Harding's 'Wild Track', which brought something new to an ancient and universal theme. As well as being deeply moved by her beautiful writing, we found the aural emphasis of the piece revelatory and inspiringly different from the usual focus on the visual sense in this genre.

It was an enjoyable challenge to select the pieces for this anthology from an outstanding longlist, so many of which deserve a special mention. But we worked to meet the aim of the prize in seeking 'engaging, unique, essay-length non-fiction that responds to the time we are in and the world as it is, challenging established notions of nature writing where necessary'. We very much hope that these works of new nature writing by emerging and talented writers will move, provoke and ultimately inspire readers, as they did all of us.

MARCHELLE FARRELL
September 2024

THE WINNING ESSAY

MATT SOWERBY

HOPE IS THE THING WITH FLIPPERS

It's 5:30 pm on 20th June 2019, and London's Natural History Museum is closing for the night, when the building will be used for a private party celebrating the UK's petroleum industry.

Crowds stream past thousands of beady-eyed taxidermy specimens into Hintze Hall, under the vast blue whale skeleton, out of the gaping doors, and onto the front lawn.

Many glance back at the whale, suspended mid-lunge in the centre of the hall, diving forever after them.

They're all being gently cajoled to hurry up by the museum staff, who just about hear the buzz of climate activists gathering on the front lawn with their placards.

The most striking thing about the whale skeleton, other than it belonging to the largest creature ever to have existed, is how much it and Hintze Hall resemble each other – the one fitting inside the other like *matryoshka* dolls.

The whale's open mouth lines up perfectly with the museum's double doors. Her bones are the same light brown as the marble walls. Her flippers reach out towards the east and west wings of the museum. Her tail rises in parallel with the grand staircase at the hall's far end. Even the columns begin to feel a bit like a rib cage.

Against every logic, the skeleton's presence feels almost natural. It also feels like you're somehow inside a whale.

The security guard has half an eye on a group of teenagers, twenty maybe, probably part of a school trip, who are dragging their feet on their way out of the museum. Pushing their luck.

Just then, the teenagers move as one into the centre of the hall, crouching down on the cold marble floor, arms linking into a chain.

Hintze Hall is now under occupation.

The whale beached near Wexford, Ireland during a storm in March 1891. A young lifeboat pilot named Ned Wickham put her out of her misery, harpooning her with a long knife attached to a stick.[1]

Recent isotope analysis reveals she had just spent almost a year in warm waters, likely nursing a calf. But at the time of her death, she was alone.

The whale's body rotted on a beach for two months before it was transported to the Museum. It wasn't until the 1930s that they found a room big enough for her, by which point the blue whale population was practically extinct outside Antarctica

– and probably didn't have long left there either.

I can't think of much as hopeless as a dead blue whale, or a beached one slowly suffocating under its own weight. But in 2017, when the museum moved the skeleton to Hintze Hall, they decided to give her the name 'Hope': a symbol 'for the future of the natural world'.[2]

There is something violent about giving a name to a whale. The word 'whale' has the sound of a kind of hopeless cry; a *wail*. It is both a noun and a verb: used to identify an animal and also to name the act of killing it. Historically, for a whale to be named was for it to be marked for death, and many of the names we give to whale species have a deathliness about them too: narwhal means 'corpse whale'; orcas are named after the Roman god of the underworld; right whales earned their name by being the 'right whale' to kill; and other species like Minke, Bryde's or Omaru are all named in honour of particularly successful whalers.[3]

Flinging a whale's name from his crow's nest, a whaling captain would establish the trajectory of the harpoon which would then fire. Enclosing a wild whale into human language was always the first step towards enclosing it in the hull of a ship.

Still, I came to the Natural History Museum looking for hope. Through its name, this whale promised it.

HOPE IS THE THING WITH FLIPPERS

I have mixed feelings about the phrase 'eco-anxiety'. It reminds me a little of 'opiophobia', a phrase coined in the 1990s by US pharmaceutical companies: 'Stop being so afraid of prescribing opioids,' doctors were told. 'What is with all this opiophobia?'

In 2019 the multi-billion pharmaceutical company Purdue Pharma declared bankruptcy following decades of litigation. Prosecutors argued that Purdue was knowingly fuelling an opioid epidemic through the aggressive and inaccurate marketing of their painkiller OxyContin. Thousands might still be alive if society had been more opiophobic.[4]

I worry that calling it 'eco-anxiety' somehow makes it seem irrational. I worry it makes it seem like 'my issue' when climate change affects all of us.

At the same time, I know most people don't think about climate change as much as I do. Even if they should. Even if they understand the problem.

It started in January 2019, the day of Greta Thunberg's 'Our House is on Fire' speech:

> Adults keep saying: 'We owe it to the young people to give them hope.' But I don't want your hope. I don't want you to be hopeful. I want you to panic. I want you to feel the fear I feel every day. And then I want you to act. I want you to act as you would in a crisis. I want you to act as if our house is on fire. Because it is.[5]

Suddenly, climate change stopped feeling distant.

People trapped in a house on fire react in one of three ways: some try to tackle the flames directly; some try to escape; and some find themselves completely unable to move, just watching the blaze approach.

Fight, flight, freeze.

In the months after Greta's speech, with nowhere to fly to, I fought.

I skipped school and went to my first protest, and then my second, and then my third. I wrote articles, and poems, and speeches. I signed petitions, and sent emails, and ran workshops, and read books, and led marches.

And then, finally, I burnt out.

The word 'eco' comes from the Greek *oikos*, meaning 'house'. The word 'anxiety' comes from the Latin *angere*, meaning 'choking'. So people with eco-anxiety are choking on the smoke of their own homes.

Maybe panic inspires action, but it isn't meant to last very long and when it does there are consequences. The word comes from *Pan*, the name of a nature god who could just scream all his problems away. Pan is also one of the only gods in Greek mythology who dies.

The conservationist Aldo Leopold wrote back in 1949 that 'One of the penalties of an ecological education is that one lives alone in a world of wounds.'[6]

HOPE IS THE THING WITH FLIPPERS

Something about that hits, although I know I'm not really 'alone': according to one study from 2021, 84 per cent of 16–25 year olds globally experience climate anxiety.[7]

Still, climate change brings such fresh grief – so fresh most of the dying hasn't even happened yet. Often the only way to function, seemingly the only practical option, is to get on with business as usual. And then there's the guilt in knowing that 'business as usual' is what is causing the dying in the first place.

Temperatures warmed; I froze.

So six months after Greta's speech, I went against her wishes. I arrived at the Natural History Museum determined to find Hope: a blue whale diving towards me, mouth open, ready to swallow me whole.

The truth is, blue whales aren't actually that blue. In 1682, the Scottish physician Robert Sibbald described one 78-foot male that washed up near the ancient fortress at Abercorn to be mostly black but with a white belly. His was the first ever scientific description of a blue whale, which was initially named 'Sibbald's Rorqual' after him.[8]

When Hope beached, her skin was described as a mixture of black, slate, green, and white, with only the flippers showing a hint of blue.

For most of whaling history, no one had a good idea what blue whales looked like. No one hunted them because they were too fast to catch and too big to do anything with. That all changed on Christmas Eve 1868, when the Norwegian whaling captain Svend Foyn patented the exploding harpoon, soon followed by the first steam-powered whaling ship. For the first time, it became possible to hunt, and therefore truly see, a blue whale. It was the beginning of modern whaling.[9]

Six years later, a Norwegian scientist proposed that since *Balaenoptera musculus* 'seen at a distance, has a very distinctly bluish cast', the animal should be commonly referred to as *Blåhval*. Sars credited the idea to Foyn.[10]

Like other cetaceans, then, the blue whale's name is deathly: the man who gave the whales their blueness is the same man who kickstarted their destruction.

By the time a moratorium on hunting blue whales was introduced in 1966, the global population had dropped from 250,000 to only 400.[11]

In 1982, this moratorium was extended to cease all commercial whaling among signatory nations. It was something no one had thought possible, until it happened. Most historians draw a connection between the policy – the near destruction of a once-powerful industry – and a grassroots movement to 'Save the Whales' which had rapidly gained in popularity around the world.[12]

HOPE IS THE THING WITH FLIPPERS

Since then, amazingly, the global population of blue whales has risen back up to about 20,000. This is the story that prompted the Natural History Museum to give their blue whale skeleton the name 'Hope'.

By pure coincidence, it turns out that Foyn's whaling ship, the first ship fast enough to chase and kill a blue whale, was named *Spes et Fides* – 'Hope and Confidence'.[13] I find other whaling ships named *Hope*: one from Liverpool made a grand total of five voyages, and there's an *SS Hope* on which Arthur Conan Doyle served as ship's surgeon and harpooner.[14]

Whaling was dangerous, and it is understandable that crews and investors might have felt the need to name a ship '*Hope*' as a kind of good-luck charm: another *Hope*, harboured at Peterhead, was one of eighteen whaling vessels lost in 1830. Another Peterhead whaler was named *Hope* in its honour.[15]

I try to get my head around it: decades ago, blue whales were destined for extinction and the only symbols of hope in the picture were the ships being used to destroy them. Now, the work of environmental activists has made the same species into a symbol of hope for the entire planet in one of the world's most famous museums.

Hintze Hall, the entrance and heart of the Natural History Museum, was designed as a

'Cathedral of Nature' complete with towers, columns, a cruciform floor plan and three large stained-glass windows at the far end.

The room is overrun with gargoyles and skeletons – creatures of stone and bone. Terracotta monkeys climb the pillars, fossil fish swim through the walls, and extinct giants stand guard in the archways.

The ceiling is painted with plants in gold frames like the pages of a herbarium, each with its Latin name along the bottom. It is called the 'Gilded Canopy', and the plants were selected based on their importance to the British Empire. I spot *Gossypium herbaceum*, *Nicotiana tabacum*, and *Saccharum officinarum* side by side: cotton, tobacco, sugarcane.

In *The Secret Life of Books*, Tom Mole writes:

> A library is an argument. An argument about [...] what kinds of things belong together, about what's more important and what's less so. The books that we choose to keep, the ones that we display most prominently, and the ones that we shelve together make an implicit claim about what we value and how we perceive the world.[16]

The same is true of museums – maybe especially the Natural History Museum where words like 'natural' and 'scientific' are used in abundance to suggest that the messages we are given are objective. The creation of the museum was funded from the profits of the British Empire, partly to demonstrate the diversity of wildlife found in it, but also to assert its power and ability to dominate by killing, collecting and scientifically categorising examples of so many lifeforms.[17]

The Gilded Canopy is a reminder that Natural History collections in Europe were often closely tied to the development and popularisation of Scientific Racism and Eugenics – the flimsy biological theories used to justify much of the politics and economics of the colonies, including racial slavery. These theories were 'evidenced' using human remains kept and displayed in Western collections.

The Museum's own founder Richard Owen wrote that 'No collection of Zoology can be regarded as complete that does not contain illustrations of the physical or natural history characters of the human' and that 'The skeletons of every variety ought to be arranged side by side for facility of comparison.'[18]

According to a Freedom of Information request, the Natural History Museum still has the remains of about 12,000 people of colour in their collection – something they don't seem to talk about elsewhere.[19]

Today Owen is best remembered as the leading critic of Darwin's Theory of Evolution, and Owen's scepticism may also have influenced the design of Hintze Hall. Owen instructed Waterhouse to place extinct species on the East of Hintze Hall, and living or 'extant' species on the West. The theory is that, by placing extant species in a different area to their distant ancestors, Owen was encouraging visitors not to dwell on any family resemblances.[20]

I realise I have no idea who Hintze Hall is named after. He could have been some Victorian natural historian, or perhaps a modern environmentalist – the museum also has an Attenborough Suite. I google it.

Michael Hintze is a billionaire asset manager, political donor, and member of the House of Lords. He is also a Trustee to a right-wing economic think tank and lobbying group called the Institute of Economic Affairs – an organisation associated (correctly or incorrectly) with the rise of both Margaret Thatcher and Liz Truss.

In 2009 Hintze was one of three wealthy IEA Trustees to fund Nigel Lawson, Thatcher's Chancellor of the Exchequer, to set up another lobbying group called the Global Warming Policy Foundation (GWPF).[21] This group's focus was to obfuscate the consensus established by the world's leading climate scientists and to slow down the energy transition. Unsurprisingly, the GWPF also receives funding from the fossil fuel industry.[22]

HOPE IS THE THING WITH FLIPPERS

Two years after the press discovered Hintze's dealings in the GWPF, he made a £5 million donation to the Natural History Museum.[23] This money paid for Hope to be moved, restored, repositioned and re-exhibited in the building's entrance.

One condition: the museum's Central Hall would need to be renamed.[24]

Every year, 5 million people, mostly children, visit the Natural History Museum and learn to associate the Hintze name with the blue whale skeleton – a 'symbol of hope for the future of the natural world', rather than with his dealings with the GWPF.

I came to the museum looking for hope, and found her with a name-shaped harpoon in her back. I remember Greta: 'I don't want you to be hopeful. I want you to panic.'

I left.

How do I build a home in a house on fire?

How do I live alone in a world of wounds?

How do I save the whale on my chest?

Michael Hintze's donation is not the only oil-stained money the Natural History Museum has accepted.

From 1989 to 2019, the museum hosted annual black-tie awards dinners for the UK's petroleum industry. For thirty years the biggest names in oil would gather in Hintze Hall, each table sponsored by a different fossil fuel company that would either award tickets to their employees as incentives, or to potential partners they wanted to shmooze.[25]

The extravagance of these events went up and down over the years with the price of oil, but normally free champagne would be offered at the door, and drinks from the bar could be charged on the company tab.

What never changed were the sharp suits, fine dresses and kilts (a lot of the industry is based in Aberdeen), the lavish steaks and canapés, and the raffle where petroleum geologists could win fossils as prizes. Then a keynote speaker would give a presentation and hand out the awards.

For decades, a life-size plaster-cast skeleton called Dippy the Diplodocus watched over these events, posing for photo after photo. Then, in 2017, Dippy was replaced by Hope.

I can't picture the petroleum dinners at the Natural History Museum without picturing a cartoon published by *Vanity Fair* in 1861.[26] It is a fever dream of an image: whales in long tailcoats and ballgowns dance and gossip, drinking champagne from long flutes. A particularly stylish cetacean glances at the viewer from behind a monocle. The cartoon was titled 'A Grand Ball Given by the Whales in Honor of the Discovery of the Oil Wells in Pennsylvania'. The banners have slogans like 'Oils well that ends well' and 'We wail no more for our blubber'. It was published two years after the dawn of the petroleum industry.

Many of the uses we have for petroleum today, such as street lighting, machine lubrication and weapons manufacture, once used whale oil. At one point, the term 'the oil industry' actually referred to whaling, and even if the 'cars' of Victorian England were powered by horses, the whips were whalebone. Over time, the oil of living sea creatures was substituted with the oil of those that died long ago. Many of the commodities we now make out of plastic, from suitcases to clothing or cosmetics, were once formed out of the bodies of whales too.[27]

When the petroleum industry was born in Pennsylvania in 1859, it was another blow against an industry already struggling from depleted stocks and that would soon be targeted by Confederates in the Civil War.[28]

Today, the petroleum industry and their friends sometimes like to tell this story: how petroleum saved the whales. They leave out how the growth of the petroleum industry led to a series of technological advancements within the whaling industry, not least diesel-powered whaling ships, that saved whaling from the brink. We soon discovered new uses for whale bodies. Whaling didn't peak until the 1960s.[29]

The *Vanity Fair* cartoon feels especially dystopian given the danger petroleum poses to whales today in the form of oil spills, plastic pollution, seismic testing, and climate change. It's not clear if the 'Grand Ball' is on land or underwater, and I wonder if these are whales dressed as humans, or humans masked as whales.

The petroleum dinners at the Natural History Museum were organised by the Geological Society of London – one of the oldest and best-respected scientific societies in the world. Richard Owen was a member of the Geological Society, as is David Attenborough today.

But by the late 2010s, the internal influence of the Society's 'Petroleum Group' had grown massively, and climate denial with it. Membership among academics was falling sharply, leaving only 'industry geologists' holding the reins.[30] Nick Rogers, the President at the time, remembers an open letter from some Society Fellows in 2018, arguing against anthropogenic causes of climate change, and over the next two years, several members resigned in protest of the Society's relationship with the oil and gas industry.

The most generous 'Platinum Level' donors were BP and Halliburton – two companies involved in the Deepwater Horizon Oil Spill in 2010. At the 'Gold Level' were TotalEnergies, Bluewater Offshore, Dana Petroleum, and two non-fossil fuel organisations: the mining group Rio Tinto and the UK Government's Nuclear Waste Services. The list of Silver- and Bronze-Level Patrons was also mostly made up of oil companies, as well as the lawyers, consultants, accountants and technology firms that specialise in supporting them. These are the organisations that would party together every year in the Natural History Museum, surrounded by fossils of species long extinct, and taxidermy specimens of species that their work continues to endanger.

But as the petroleum industry arrived at the museum in 2019, they found five hundred activists, mostly families, gathered on the front lawn for a picnic – a Dinner of Hope in protest of what the activists were calling the Dinner of Extinction.[31]

Most party guests slip in through the side door, so they don't get a good look at the forest of placards, banners, flags, drums, megaphones, and cameras – although it is difficult to miss the giant pink dodo towering over everything.

Some protestors balance tiny whales on their knees, hand-stitched out of old jeans. Many Senegalese activists wear green, yellow and red flags in support of corruption charges being brought against BP in their country. Someone has set up a vegan buffet on a giant pink picnic blanket, and someone else has cordoned off a kids' play area called 'The Natural Futures Museum' next to a giant cutout of a blue whale.[32]

Inside the museum, Hintze Hall is still being held hostage by a group of teenagers, huddling in the shadow of the whale.

There are a few museum staff who have been hurriedly called in to play diplomat, a few security guards worried that they might be asked to wrestle a child, and a couple of lefty journalists who have snuck in to conduct interviews. Occasionally a chant breaks out:

> *They made their money putting carbon in the air*
> *They wrecked our futures and we're here to declare*
> *We are the youth and they're stepping on our rights*
> *We are the youth and we're fighting for our lives.*[33]

The teenagers have three demands for the museum: cancel the Petroleum Group's dinner; declare a climate and ecological emergency; and cut any and all ties with the fossil fuel industry. The Natural History Museum has refused all of them.[34]

'I learnt about the threat that is humanity's effect on the planet right here in this building,' one teenager tells a cameraman, 'and I think it's beautiful that we are all here in solidarity with Hope above us, and with each other, to share the message of the Natural History, and hopefully Future, Museum.'

I pause the video and think about that word: 'solidarity'. Maybe I was expecting the activists to tear apart the whale skeleton bone from bone, renouncing it as Michael Hintze's monument of greenwash and false hope. How can you have solidarity with a skeleton? With that skeleton?

And then it clicks that this isn't Hintze's Hall any more. It is theirs.

And it's not just the Hall that the activists have chosen to claim for themselves – it is the whale, and it is hope.

Hope is a word used incorrectly too often when we talk about the environment. It makes sense that Greta Thunberg was so suspicious of it. Often hope is described as a *thing*.

'"Hope" is the *thing* with feathers,' wrote the poet Emily Dickinson.[35]

'Hope is the thing with flippers,' I think, and then I remember the last stanza of that poem:

I've heard it in the chillest land,
And on the strangest sea;
Yet, never, in Extremity,
It asked a crumb of me.

Hope promises everything, and demands not a crumb. It is something to find, something to reassure us that the world might still work out OK. And half the time when you grab hold of this kind of hope, it disappears in your hands. Because no one has more cause to manufacture false hope than those trying their hardest to destroy the possibility of a better world.

But there's another kind of hope, I realise.

Hope as a verb. Hope as a doing word. Hope reclaimed.

Greta Thunberg has stopped telling people 'I don't want you to hope,' and started saying instead that 'Hope is taking action.'[36]

Occupying Hope.

Occupying the museum, the whale, the word.

Hope as being fourteen and terrified but refusing to leave, sweaty arms linked with friends and strangers, surrounded by security guards and unsure what the consequences of any of this will be – all so you can shout loud enough for every petroleum industry employee, representative and executive swarming the building to hear:

> *We are the youth and they're stepping on our rights*
> *We are the youth and we're fighting for our lives.*

HOPE IS THE THING WITH FLIPPERS

The Natural History Museum never publicly relented to any of the young activists' demands. The Petroleum Group of the Geological Society still had their awards dinner in the museum, just in a smaller room.

Then, a few months later, the museum announced they were declaring a Planetary Emergency, and at the same time cutting their last ties with the fossil fuel industry.[37]

It was also decided that, for the first time in thirty years, the Petroleum Group's next annual awards dinner would not take place in the museum. Since 2020, these dinners have taken place in Aberdeen, and the Petroleum Group has renamed itself 'the Energy Group'.[38]

Rebecca Solnit writes 'Your opponents would love you to believe that you have no power, that there's no reason to act, that you can't win.'[39]

Every one of the activists' demands was met within a year, but quietly enough to go almost unnoticed. The Natural History Museum presented each as their own idea. It was like the museum didn't want word getting out that they would ever bend to protestors – they knew better than to give activists too much hope.

I've started going more regularly to see the whale. Hintze Hall has not been renamed. It still bothers me that he has this claim over her – that this incredibly public association exists between Hope and the Hintze name.

But I know these issues can be overcome with action, and I make a point to tell everyone I meet who Hintze really is, and what really happened here.

I remind myself that the reason there are no more whaling ships called 'Hope' but that there is at least one whale that *is*, is because of people choosing to take action. It makes me want to be brave.

I look up at the whale skeleton, suspended in mid-lunge. She looks so lifelike: entirely still and yet diving with such purpose. It should feel like ventriloquism but somehow it doesn't, perhaps because I know this skeleton is representative of 20,000 living blue whales diving like her but after plankton, not dustmotes.

At the same time, I know she is dead. I know it was horrible. And I know there is so much dying to come that could have been avoided — human as well as animal. But I need to actively grieve that. And coming to this Natural History mausoleum gives me a little time and space to feel everything that is happening, and think through what I want to do about it.

The whale also has the strange effect of making the entire museum feel underwater. I'm reminded that when a whale dies at sea, its decomposing body creates an oasis on the bottom of the ocean that can

HOPE IS THE THING WITH FLIPPERS

last for decades. It becomes an ecosystem in itself, a source of life.

At the same time, I'm transported into a future of sea level rise. London isn't safe, and no imaginary future oasis could ever make up for losing what we have. But it's certainly a reminder to look for the good that comes with the bad. A blue whale is only blue if you're looking for it to be.

The last time I went to the Natural History Museum, I had something particular in mind. I'd watched an interview with the Museum's Curator of Mammals, where he said something cryptic about Hope:

> There's a reason why we've hung her with one flipper slightly up, one flipper slightly down, a little bit of rotation in the tail vertebrae, the way the head is positioned... let's see if people can see what she's doing.[40]

I had never thought of Hope as anything other than symmetrical, but looking again I could just about see what he meant. It took me three full rotations of the hall before it clicked.

The whale isn't diving directly forward, she's *turning*. She's turning to the right.

And I remembered Richard Owen's plans to have living species represented on one side of the hall and extinct species on the other. And I wondered if this might be the best definition for hope: not the belief that everything can be or is going to be OK, but – despite that – the decision to actively turn towards life.

THE SHORTLISTED ESSAYS

NIELLAH ARBOINE

INTO EACH LIFE, SOME RAIN MUST FALL

Since leaving the city and turning thirty, I haven't stopped crying. I welled up while feeding the chickens the other morning. The autumnal air clung to the inside of my lungs like something sticky, reminding me that the colder months were coming to visit again. A rendition of 'I'm Not in Love' sung by Kelsey Lu came on shuffle, as I chucked pellets mixed with crushed seashells from old jam jars into the coop. And the silky crescendo of *Big boys don't cry, big boys don't cry* echoed from my headphones like a mockery.

The chickens pecked around my feet, cooing and squawking as my face stung with heat. Soon the sticky cold in my lungs became lodged in my throat instead. Tears tumbled and I stood there in the chicken shit with a chorus of mini-feathered dinosaurs circling and keeping me company as I made nostalgia in real time.

This sort of crying has become a common occurrence since moving to a farm early last year. The day I left London, my friend picked me up from the house and I closed the door for the last time

INTO EACH LIFE, SOME RAIN MUST FALL

on the memories it held. We shoved Ikéa bags and tattered boxes into the car and drove off. It rained heavily, and soon the blur of the city sped by us and like watercolour, the view smudged from greens to rich browns drowning in the rain. We eventually approached an empty flooded country road, she slowed the car to a crawl and we peeked at each other. 'My new ends,' I muttered and we laughed.

Months later and settled in, it didn't take much to make me cry, including in the company of chickens. I thought about my grandma's chickens in Jamaica and whether they were the same breed as the ones I was stifling snotty tears around. Both were brown, the same size and lay tan freckled eggs. But then I reminded myself that the chickens probably didn't care, so why should I?

On a recent trip to visit my grandma, I watched her, well into her eighties, scaling down the limestone underbelly of her house – a big pit of a gully. What seemed like certain death for most her age, or at least an expensive hip replacement, was light work for my grandma. She was as nimble as the rooster, who due to his male privilege got to roam the crevasses of the rocks, yelling at anyone who would listen to him, coconut trees, the locked-up hens or us. My grandma knew each foot placement like a psalm and where to hold the steel rods that poked out of the earth like chin whiskers for balance. I'm sure if she had to, she could do it with her eyes closed. I'd clamber down after her, sweaty, cautious and clumsy until we reached the coop. Grandma showed me where the feed lived in a big blue barrel, the hose to refill their water, and how to climb up the small handmade ladder to collect the eggs, sometimes still warm, but always tacked with young feathers.

Since moving, I've been learning to have a kinship with chickens and other members of the more-than-human world I've struggled to respect, let alone love, before. I felt like a stubborn child being dragged through my own undoing. Not too long ago, while I was cleaning out one of their beds, an overly excited hen got her talons lodged in my coat from behind. We both screamed and flapped in our own languages. From the front, perhaps it looked like I had wings.

And when all twelve hens stopped laying for six weeks, I had to quieten my childish rage. What was the point of these chickens, I thought, if they couldn't do their only job, provide eggs for us to eat? Why was I moisturising their knobbly feet with Vaseline every time they got mites on their legs? But chickens didn't have jobs; their purpose wasn't to feed me; they didn't sign up to be workers; and if they never laid another egg that was okay. With age, I find I'm constantly catching my projections.

INTO EACH LIFE, SOME RAIN MUST FALL

When the most recent cohort of chickens first arrived in the back of a car from the battery farm in the spring, their feathers barely covered their pink skin. I realised that now in their twilight years, this was probably the first time they saw sunlight. Chickens experience rapid eye movement when they sleep, just like we do. They might not dream in the exact same way, but they do dream. I held one for the first time around then. The only other times I'd had my hands around a chicken, it was plucked and stiff with a sort of rigor mortis fresh from the morgues of Lidl. This one, she was warm and velvet.

Wasps were next on my agenda. My disdain for them was venomous and justified. Wasps were a terror, stinging without rhyme or reason, put on the planet to agitate me personally. They didn't even make honey and at least bees had the decency to die in their stinging kamikaze strikes.

At a festival on a particularly overcast weekend in the summer, a friend spat a wasp out onto the trodden grass. It drowned trying to drink from her cup and its corpse ended up swirling into her mouth. We all laughed and ran in small circles, giddy and frightened every time a wasp stalked our cups of sugary cocktails. But I'd end up being the only victim that weekend. While I was swaying to jazz crooners, a pain shot through the bottom of my left middle finger. I dropped my cup and screamed profanities, cursing the wasp and its whole lineage.

My summer felt especially imprinted by wasps. All late August, giant hornets flew out of the light fixtures in my attic room, a common place for wasps to make their nests. Fear mixed with anger took me on a different path: why not get to know them, and learn to be in community with them? After all, they were here first, by millions of years.

I learned that wasps didn't evolve in the same way bees did; bees had far better PR. During the winter months, one by one wasps die off, leaving the queen hibernating. And now with no laying queen, the workers' symbiotic relationship with the larvae, who produce sugary spit for them in exchange for chewed-up insects, comes to an end. On their slow march to death, the wasps buzz around confused, irritated and hungry – drunk on the last of the summer fruits while they wait to leave this world.

I saw the autumn and winter on the farm as a living graveyard. A wasp sat parched on a table in the nursery as I propagated some straggly thyme. Another embedded himself into a rotten apple stuck on the roof of the chicken coop. I found one more on the tarmac, I ran inside and put some granulated sugar and water on a teaspoon, but by the time I made my way back, the wasp was gone. And on my small bedroom window a hornet too tired to fly ascended my turquoise plant pot. The wasp didn't

INTO EACH LIFE, SOME RAIN MUST FALL

fight when I caught her between a glass and a postcard with a rainbow and a beaming sun with the words 'nothing really matters' on it.

Only female wasps sting. I thought about them in a different light after that. Sometimes fear forces you to protect yourself the only way you know how. I got stung again some months after my last painful encounter with a wasp while sitting at my desk painting. A small, darting throb echoed through my toe. I must have accidentally put my foot on the drowsy wasp. Weak and disorientated, even in her last moments, she still mustered up the energy to protect what little life she had left. She might be gone, but a part of her lives in me – her peptides and enzymes making alchemy with my blood. The pain reminded me I'm alive, and that life will always be worth fighting for. I apologised and thanked her.

So, I'm learning to love what I thought I couldn't. I believed I'd never be able to fall into love in this way. I'd always be apprehensively dipping my toe into the swell of glitter and gold, watching others jump, drown, backstroke and dive into love around me. But I couldn't. Falling in love was like trying to catch smoke, or remember a disappearing dream.

But I think I found love, or at least chose love. I'm reminded of the words of bell hooks: 'When we choose to love we choose to move against fear – against alienation and separation. The choice to love is the choice to connect – to find ourselves in the other.' And the words of Toni Morrison: 'I didn't fall in love, I rose in it.'

I learned to love the farm dog, although I'd never had pets growing up, beyond the occasional goldfish. He made me feel brave on our countryside walks. When I curled into myself, fearing the danger that comes with the rural idyll for someone who looks like me, with him by my side, I unfurled. He kept me company, telling me we'd be alright with every nudge and sniff as we trudged through the public footpaths.

I chose to love a tree at the front of the farm near a small hidden meadow. I loved friends who showed me care wasn't transactional. It was easier to be soft on this farm than my previous decades living in the surge of an oftentimes, unforgiving city. No screams of the Jubilee tube line slicing through me. No more suspicion of everything and everyone, giving me no choice but to harden. But just like the soil in spring, I became soft again.

Before moving, I found myself saying or thinking or wishing *I just want to live up a tree*. Whenever I was overwhelmed by the world crumbling around me, or stressed by work, or watching most of the money tumble out of my bank into the hands of a cruel landlord, I would repeat, *I just want to live up a tree*.

INTO EACH LIFE, SOME RAIN MUST FALL

Feeling surveilled and othered for my whole life, before I even had the language for it, had stiffened me. It's a chore to enjoy the roses when you have police accusing you of loitering in a park, which I'd imagine is the most ideal place to loiter. Aged sixteen, we all scarpered in different directions one afternoon after finishing school, a scatter of desire lines taking us to safety.

It was a joke at first, but it soon became a mantra of sorts. If I could just live up a tree then the growing triangle of black mould speckled like stars on the living room wall wouldn't matter anymore. If I could find some respite up a tree then perhaps I wouldn't have to think about my relationship that was clumsily held together by nostalgia and good intentions. If I could just live up any tree, I'd be safe from the clutches of a hardening and selfish society that saw nuance as deviance. If I could live up a tree, maybe I could eventually be a part of a tree – stretch marks melting into the hard grooves of bark, veins matching the dark green veins of leaves, limbs dancing with the spinning helicopter seeds of the sycamore.

I thought of those times with my grandma when my soil softened. A few years before moving to the farm, I remembered walking down to the local cluster of shops in the scorching afternoon heat, not far from her house and rowdy chickens. It was the same road I walked down as a child, and perhaps one my grandma journeyed down in her youth too long before the roads were tarmacked. The air smelt moist, exactly how I remembered it, pulling me back to those early years in my life when I felt so held by the land.

Children in neat, starched khaki-coloured uniforms chatted away as they began to stroll up the path from school. An old lady sat on her veranda gazed out at nothing in particular. And trucks zoomed by with young men in vests barely clinging on as they vanished into the distant folds of the snaking road flanked by greenery. On walks like that one, I thought about how much of a curious warmth it was to be surrounded by people who looked like me.

I stopped and looked over the road's edge into the endless mouth of the breathing gully, thinking about how my eyes could never meet the horizon in London. There was always an obstacle blocking it. Bricks, fences, cranes, steel, glass, people.

There with my grandma, I blurred into everyone and everything. I melted into our shared brown tones. I merged with the bamboo leaves and the line of biting red ants. I blended into the doctor bird's impossibly fast wings and the hard, black seeds of the creamy ackee fruit. I melted with the ripples of water and smooth stones lining the river's bed. I softened in Jamaica.

INTO EACH LIFE, SOME RAIN MUST FALL

But the reality was I didn't live there, no matter how much I imagined what my life could have been like if my grandparents never left the island for a colder one. I did know that I deeply desired that comfort, of living in that figurative tree, even if perhaps naïvely. I wanted to feel as held by nature on this island as I did with my grandma on her island. Somewhere inside of me, I'd always yearned for that softened version of myself and I don't think that I was alone.

It's not perfect, but I feel that softness on this farm. This is my spring. Now, I howl at the moon, that faithful witness in the sky. I wassail the fruit trees, filling them with blessings. I give wasps their last supper and cry with the chickens. I hear music everywhere: the plop of raindrops making petrichor, the throaty coos of the wood pigeon, the wind creating *niguns* and even the light swashes of chicken feathers as they bathe in dust. These become my chants, my cantillations and cantations.

I'm not sure why I've been crying of late. My tears didn't seem like they sprouted from a nameable pain. Physiatrist Sandor Feldman believed that even happy tears aren't what we think they are. Welling up with pride when your child goes off to school for the first time isn't so much about tears of joy, but a sort of pent-up sorrow for what has been or will or could be lost – an understanding of the fleetingness and temporality of life. The child will grow up and you can't protect them from what life will throw at them. Maybe these tears of joy were just tears of delayed sadness, an understanding of our own mortality.

On a walk through the Kent countryside one Sunday afternoon, with no real plan of where I was going, my only goal being to make it back to the farm before nightfall, I burst into tears looking out at the long stretches of fields in front of me. Perhaps it was how the grass danced in the wind as the winter sun kissed each outstretched blade. Or maybe it was the blistering brightness of the cirrus-striped sky and how divine it all seemed.

But truly, I was crying because I knew it would be gone soon. I was a wanderer above the sea of fog. I think my tears of awe cloaked in sorrow were for the generations to come who may never experience the soft, clean air brushing their cheeks, a cool winter sun and a life that allows such privileges as long, pondering walks. And here I was, relishing the last embers of our burning home, a living graveyard. When I've walked into my dawn and become an ancestor, what will be left behind?

I think about my own ancestors and whether they cried those same tears for me, bitter and beautiful. Perhaps they looked out over the plantation fields they were imprisoned in and thought about

INTO EACH LIFE, SOME RAIN MUST FALL

how one day when the land had returned to itself, I could walk through them free and dreaming.

My love can feel like an inconvenience, teaching me how to divest and tread a little more quietly on the earth. My love is starting to feel like a resistance. My love hurts. My love remembers my green-fingered forebears who worked land so far from home they only had time to gift me stories and traditions passed from mouth to hand and back again.

Really, all of these tears were a libation. Tears for love and loss, and love again.

MEG BERTERA-BERWICK

THE KAILYARDS

The warm breath of manure clung in my nose. Muddy and lactic, weirdly intimate. I stopped to make sure I hadn't misread another odour: a belch of exhaust from a bus, or a ripe tang from a bin, but no. The big animal smell moseyed through the tenements, eddying at intersections, muddling through hedges. It lingered in front of the dairy-shop with its crates of empty milk bottles, drifted through my garden with its twiggy apple tree and proud shoulders of kale. The cows could have been just around the corner, grazing on the long grass by the empty bus stop. It felt like, if I walked up the road, I would find the farm tucked away behind the silent school.

Someone was obviously making a garden nearby. I was alone on the street, stooped in my own narrow garden by the cold frame, checking on the fuzzy green leaves of new mint. Every now and then, the owner of the dairy opposite would potter out to stack something, preparing for the unevenly spaced queue that would form soon. We were only a day into lockdown and the manure could amble through with such body because the gritty black gauze of pollution had already frayed in the middle.

THE KAILYARDS

No cars rushing past with a wake of fumes. No fruity ribbon of shampoo from passing commuters. Even the bus was electric, rolling quietly with no reason to stop, no black net of exhaust left to hover over the corner. If I closed my eyes, tenement and shop and city disappeared so completely that they could have just been set-dressing. Brassica leaves creaked. The freshness of mint cut jarringly through the shit. Not even the sound of cars, of the school bell, of a delivery van to splinter the immediacy of garden, field, and dung.

The smell flushed the urgency from my chest. I had woken up in the night, eyes flung wide with instant panic about what we would do, how could we prepare for this, when my brain responded, *sow a hundred plugs of radishes and parsley*. I laughed at myself in the dark but the feeling of it still propelled me outside in the morning. Like every day, I had set the heavy watering can on the low stone wall and swung my leg over. I moved through the garden as if doing laps through a pool: pushing off the wall with my watering can, darting down towards the bench as I watered, back towards the cold frame to check on the seedlings, back again to the compost with a handful of baby slugs. It felt important not to stand still too long. My garden, only 2.5 metres wide and 5 metres long, was a thin rectangle of liminal space between my flat and the pavement. I surreptitiously hugged the windows when anyone passed, under the guise of inspecting the irises on the windowsill.

My laps slowed down until I was standing still, sniffing. The manure was closer to me than any stranger had been for weeks. It lingered all morning and into the afternoon. I smelt it on the back step at night, cut through with the vegetal ding of growing grass and wet mud. I walked through it with my dog in the unnervingly quiet mornings, got caught in the weird embrace of it in the garden after lunch. Eventually it stopped feeling like an interloper.

That week, article after article pointed gingerly to the collapsing supply chains that made people so frightened of food shortages that they were buying seed in bulk. The media described the phenomenon as a resurgence of wartime victory gardens; places of temporary, alternative subsistence. But the gardens I saw emerge overnight around tenements and flats did not have the utilitarian urgency of victory gardens, or even the hoarding arrogance of preppers; they were small, earnest, warmly idiosyncratic. Each one a fervent fruiting body of the same concerned impulse. In them, the ground seemed to blink with wakefulness, twitching back its concrete skin to release a fug of well-rotted shit and sweet grassiness, remembering itself.

*

THE KAILYARDS

'The village or hamlet of Langside consists of some score or so of houses, principally one-storeyed cottages, clustering irregularly amidst patches of garden, and finely screened by fruit and other trees.' The Langside that Glasgow writer Hugh MacDonald visited in the early 1850s was still in the parish of Cathcart, in the county of Renfrewshire, more than forty years away from being incorporated into the city of Glasgow. His impressions in the 1854 collection *Rambles Round Glasgow* are of a place I cannot navigate: where the village clustered at the top of the slope and the view looked out over rolling hills, the White Cart Water blinking along the holm, stone kirks rising from their wooded settlements. 'Like most other Scottish villages, it seems to have been left in a great measure to "hing as it grew", and consequently it possesses a picturesqueness of aspect to which our more regularly constructed modern towns are utter strangers.'

The 1859 Ordnance Survey (OS) map of Renfrewshire draws the shape of this Langside in pink and beige. The heart of it is a short twig of an avenue with cottages joined up in long rows on either side; not completely unlike the tenements today and yet the only thing recognisable to me was the shape these streets make, a pointed oblong like a piece of quartz. As MacDonald says, the gardens are numerous, a dozen or so stretching in long rows or huddling in squat rectangles behind the cottages. The mapmaker has drawn little perforated lines of paths and scribbled wee bushes and trees through them. They are different altogether to the gardens that surround the named villas sitting at the edges of the village. Those gardens are large and symmetrical; it's implied that they would be ornate in their straight lines and elegant curves. They do not clump or meander the way the kailyards do.

'The majority of the inhabitants are weavers, who manage to make ends meet better than the generality of their City brethren, by the cultivation, during spare hours, of their bits of kailyard, the produce of which adds materially to the comfort of their families.' (MacDonald) Sometime in the previous millennium, cultivated kale and cabbage were introduced to lowland Scotland by European settlers, likely Roman invaders or Cistercian monk colonisers. When MacDonald wrote in the 1850s, it was foundational to most meals. 'Kail' meant many things: *green kail* meant the *Brassica oleracea acephela* we know as kale today but *bow kail* might mean heading cabbage. The kail worm was the cabbage white caterpillar that ate brassicas down to lace veins; the kail gully was the knife that cut the kale; the kail pot was where the broth was made; the kail-bell was the dinner bell; 'kail' was your dinner, and sometimes it was muslin kail (broth made of water,

THE KAILYARDS

barley, and greens) or it was pan kail (broth made of kale cut very small, thickened with a little oatmeal and butter or lard) or maybe kailkenny (potatoes and cabbage or kale mashed together with cream).

The kailyard was the garden. As a place and as a concept, it sat somewhere between the domestic and the agricultural, where the monotony of porridge in the pot and grain in the field was broken up with the vivacity of green things. In 1813, the writer Patrick Neill published a report on Scotland's gardens for the Board of Agriculture, in which he paid particular attention to the content and use of kailyards by working class cottagers. He lists the vegetables that were most commonly grown ('cabbages, pease, beans, potatoes, turnips, onions, leeks, and carrots', mustard for condiment, chives, maybe 'a little sallad' like parsley and common cress), the soft fruits ('rows of gooseberries are not infrequent; and against the walls of the cottage next the garden are commonly placed some red or white currant bushes'), the trees ('an apple, pear, or cherry tree'), the most popular ornamental flowers ('common marigold, which sows itself year after year', 'white narcissus, wallflower, London pride, and polyanthuses, which the cottagers generally name *spinks*'), and the plants grown for medicine and household uses ('thyme, spearmint, and southernwood', 'rue is a general plant, being applied to any sort of ulcer, and used also as a medicine for horses', 'tansy is seldom wanting, the juice being the sovereign remedy for worms in children'.) Some plots were big enough for keeping a cow, or sowing a patch of bere, an ancient type of barley. Sometimes a bit of flax was grown for making coarse linen cloth.

I knew all this because I had wondered once what pre-industrial Scottish food was like. I found that most people will gladly tell you how grim it was, how repetitive, all that porridge and hardly any meat. Stubbornly, I could not believe that there was never a love of food in Scotland before sugar changed everything. Validation was found first in *The Scots Gard'ner*, a guide written by professional gardener John Reid in 1683; it is not so much an instruction manual as it is a manifesto on beauty and deliciousness, marrying Reid's philosophy and advice on gardening with his advice and recommendation on how to prepare the fruits and vegetables of one's labour. 'The kitchen-garden is the best of all gardens,' he says. 'Eat pickled cucumbers with roast mutton, and bake apples with sugar,' he says. 'Make a green broth with marigold, violet, and strawberry leaves.'

But the significance of the kale I found through the scavenger hunt of vegetal words – *kale, kail, colewort* – strewn through everything that the brassicas touched. They were in old songs ('The monks

THE KAILYARDS

of Melrose/made kail brose/on Fridays when they fasted'), in poetry ('To slink thro' slaps, an' reave an' steal/At stacks o' pease, or stalks o' kale!' Robert Burns), and in folk sayings ('dinna scaud yir mou wi ither fowk's kail' – don't scald your mouth with other folk's kail). They showed up carved into the architecture of late medieval churches, and cast in plaster on the ceiling of Sir Walter Scott's home, Abbotsford. Somehow, despite the ubiquity of kale in everyday life, the memory of it was considered homely, and it was not brought into the romantic refashioning of heritage Scottish food in the twentieth century.

It was not the kale so much as the vulnerability in the lockdown gardens that made me think of the kailyards. When I walked past freshly dug beds and newly sprung pots full of herbs and salad, it occurred to me that this might be the first time in more than a hundred years that so many homes in Scotland now had a subsistence garden attached. In the too-quiet mornings, I saw the static city overlaid with a double vision projected through the pastoral scents of spring: tenements displaced by the dairy farm and weavers' cottages, a grand old villa sitting in place of the Tesco Express. My street was in a field along the river, cut through by the thin line of the fast-moving mill lade. I saw the villagers' fruit trees in the apples of the churchyard and the community garden, the gooseberries in the back lane, the secret pear tree by the ugly flats.

*

My Langside garden was the largest I had ever had in my five years of growing. We chose the flat because of it, on the hottest day of the year. I wasn't even sure I would be able to make it what I wanted until the day we moved in, when I broached the idea with the landlord and he quite cheerfully gestured towards the empty pocket of gravel, 'It's all yours!' It took three trips to round up all the plants we had brought down from Inverness and stored with friends and family during the in-between time. I lined them all up against the warm sandstone wall, exhausted but giddy with relief. A place to set down all my pots, all my years of longing. I spent the first autumn looking eagerly out the window, learning the light, sketching out blueprints. In the spring, I scraped the gravel back from the low stone wall to put in four raised beds and rickety bamboo trellising.

I had envisioned it as a monastic potager in miniature: full of herbs and greens in pleasing geometric formations, enclosed by a green partition of sweet peas, climbing beans, and rampant trombocino squash. I thought the warmth of south-facing sandstone tenement would foster a microclimate, where my seedlings would have a head start and the courgettes a late finish. But the compost I used that first year was contaminated somehow; things grew, but without enthusiasm. The green partition I had dreamed of never materialised so the garden lay exposed, the opposite of private. My upstairs neighbour flicked his cigarettes into my herbs. Builders and carers left coffee cups and soda cans on the low stone wall. I saw people (men) spit into it as they passed. I planted things out far too early, during warm days in April, and they languished in the cold of May.

I had expected a glut. I had expected to be weighed down with so many courgettes that I would have to fob them off on friends and family with an apologetic but smug, 'They just keep coming!' I expected all my tender loving care, a whole season's worth of sagacious personal growth, to be reflected back at me through an overabundance of multicoloured tomatoes and kilos of purple beans. I did not expect the spring cold, or the summer gales, or the feeling that the measure of me was only as good as the garden I made.

People did compliment the garden as they passed, but it didn't look *good*, I thought, just *surprising*. I could not be convinced that it was beautiful, but I admired the cosmos when they bloomed, and the russet oranges of the Velvet Queen sunflowers. I was taken aback when one or two aubergines ripened, grown entirely outdoors. The arch trellis creaked under the weight of the trombocino squash, which had not been well-pollinated but grew anyway to something the size and length of a human leg. They were so strange that they embarrassed me a little.

When the workmen appeared at the end of September, my elderly neighbour met me in the hall and asked if I had received the letter. Letter? No? He shuffled back inside to retrieve it and I asked one of the blokes in jumpsuits if the scaffolding they were unloading was going in the front gardens as well. 'All the gardens, front and back.' Calmly, maybe a little coldly, I asked if they would delay until I had spoken to my landlord. They smoked outside and I sent a frantic email. I imagined chaos and darkness: scaffolding across the whole building, the garden crushed and lightless, access blocked for months. But an hour later, the situation had resolved itself in an anticlimactic sputter. The landlord rushed over, admitting it would have been better if he'd remembered to tell me. The workmen constructed the scaffolding around and through my arch trellis with great thoughtfulness, requiring only that a few pots be moved. Half of one window semi-blocked and the garden entrance totally obscured, but the rest of it free and clear. In some kind of cosmic compensation for my trouble, the arch trellis I had so feared would topple in a gale was now prevented from doing so, wrapped in a steel cage until November.

I felt I should have been relieved. Just a few months prior, a neighbour had put herself between the cherry tree in her tenement garden and the tree surgeon cutting it down after her landlord didn't tell her he couldn't be arsed with the upkeep. This scaffolding, really, was nothing. But despite the kindness of the workmen, the abruptness of the event registered in my body as a violation; a jarring realisation of the garden's vulnerability. Like an exposed nerve I would have to protect against the spitters, the litterers, the pedestrians who pinched off pieces of my rosemary, the drunk tweens who pulled out poles from my trellis. Like a room in my brain perpetually on display. Like a vital organ kept on the outside, aching a little at all times.

Everything died back in winter except the green shoots of garlic and the young figures of kale. I watched them shrug off the frosts, hunch stoically in the snow. They were surprisingly beautiful; I could believe, in the winter, that they had once been carved in stone in the medieval Melrose Abbey, that monks might see something in them of endurance and hope.

*

MEG BERTERA-BERWICK

I carried my camera into the garden and put my coffee on the bench at the end; my prize for completing a lap or two. It was early and cool, the bees not even in the foxgloves yet. Every other step I had to lunge over the piles of fresh garlic on the gravel path, which were meant to be drying in these warm solstice days. Soon I would hang them on the pulley clotheshorse in the bathroom, where we would live with the deepening pungency for weeks. The parsley was a short hedge of green tough stalks of flowers still shut tight, little umbels like closed fists; I took out my garden knife to cut some down, thinking I would make a stock of them and the red-veined sorrel.

As the first bumblebee motored into the borage, I clicked pillowy blue-green leaves of cavolo nero off their central stalks, piled them on top of the parsley in my colander. Patrick Neill records that this way of harvesting kale was called stooans: 'No article is in greater repute in small cottage gardens than what is styled *stooans* or *stowans*. German greens [*by which he means curly kale*] and savoys are planted early in the spring, and as they advance in growth in April, May, and June, the outer leaves are picked off, and put among broth, under the above name.' The word came from the Scots verb *stoo*, which means to cut or crop, lop or trim, whether it's the outer leaves of kale or barnyard animals' ears as a signal of ownership.

THE KAILYARDS

Learning this word felt like peeling back the cardboard from a compost bin and finding a slow worm underneath: a friendly little jolt, an unexpected transmission. In the garden, my hands were slow and careful, suddenly self-aware of their participation in the long repetition of this simple gesture. I wondered if the Langside villagers called this method stooans. I did not say the word out loud to anyone other than myself, in case it flew out more like an abomination than a resurrection. But I kept it between my front teeth as I worked, walking around other feelings without saying them either.

My partner slept on the sofa inside, limp as a rag from a run of long shifts. I tried and failed not to think about the young man he had been caring for; almost thirty, younger than us, whose mother called the Covid ICU nearly every hour. My distracted hands filled a small glass ramekin with warm red strawberries and the feeling of their juicy, seedy skin drew me, like water, into the warmth of the sun. My eyes prickled in the brightness, overcome. With no small rush of gratitude, I balanced the colander of kale on the windowsill. A quick calculation of brassicas, parsley, and woody herbs estimated I could put off a panicky trip to the grocery store for a week; until whenever the pasta and the beans ran out. I thought back to the summer before, to the great legs of squash and fingers of aubergine. I was incredulous at my own ingratitude, that I was ever so concerned with whether or not the garden was *beautiful*. When it had consoled me every day, when it had fed me tender salad leaves. We would never be self-sufficient but we had garlic, and parsley, and kale.

There was not the pressure or possibility for self-sufficiency in the kailyards either; at a time when meat was rarely consumed by working classes and most vegetables were not intensively grown in fields, the point of the kailyard was to supplement and enrich this oatmeal- and barley-heavy vegetarian diet. In 1888, the pseudonymous 'Dulsie' wrote for the *Glasgow Herald* a recollection of Langside from forty years before, in which the village 'was almost hidden away from view by garden hedges, old apple trees, and the higher Camphill'. In July and August, 'the villagers drove a brisk trade in gooseberries and apples (especially on Sundays, I am sorry to say) with the crowds of Glasgow lads and lassies.' MacDonald in his 1854 *Rambles* mentions this also: 'Several of them are famous for the quality of their gooseberries, the excellence of which during July and August tempts numerous parties from the neighbouring City.'

These must be the bushes and small trees scribbled in oval loops on the 1859 OS map. They cluster

THE KAILYARDS

tightly in the gardens that front the main road, and scatter more widely in the gardens behind. Though the boundaries between gardens on this map are marked in solid black line, and the garden paths are worn in deep fawn-coloured treads, there isn't any suggestion of how the kailyards might have been laid out: if things were grown in straight monocultural rows, or clustered in mixed groupings; if the greens were grown closer to the house or further away; if the marigolds weaved incorrigibly through the brassicas and potatoes or were kept to their own bright corners.

I gathered the kale and the herbs, pocketing gloves, feeling my packet of seed peas to count what was left. All the seed merchants were sold out, warning would-be customers that threatening emails would not speed service; how did the villagers buy their seeds, or keep them dry and cool after saving them? I wanted to know, did the gooseberries make up their hedges? Were they high enough to feel a little private, to avoid eye contact with their neighbours? Was there a gate to open from the lane, a doorway to walk through into a space enclosed by stone walls and roses, a bough with heavy apples overhanging the path?

Was my garden just a kailyard, really?

*

MEG BERTERA-BERWICK

In the dripping garden, I watched a snail travel over the grooved surface of a green tomato. There was barely room enough for me, impossible not to get a little wet brushing past lush green plants on both sides. The nasturtium had climbed over everything possible, the cold frame, the wall, the cucumbers. It was August and it wouldn't get any fuller or lusher or brighter than this. I had never had a full second year in a garden of my own before, and it moved me how each season became a dialogue of recollection, as self-seeders resurfaced in unexpected places and soil grew richer in some parts, poorer in others. I was naively wondrous about how none of it was a clean slate to start in spring, not even the pots. The ground had remembered what I did before; I remembered who I was when it threw back evidence of my inexperience; we went back and forth together in a dialogue of growth.

As I did my laps between beds, people sometimes stopped to tell me how much they liked the garden, how they wished they could do the same, but their landlords had inferred or said outright they could not. We swapped the number of years we had spent on allotment waiting lists, commiserating there weren't more, agreeing we would even tolerate the mandatory tea-time at *that one* for the joy of a half-plot. Many passers-by were surprised to learn that I rented. Their eyes flashed

THE KAILYARDS

with something I couldn't place as they voiced their reluctance to put so much money and effort into a space that they didn't own. I said that I was lucky to have this flat, to have such a considerable outdoor space during the lockdowns, that it was sheer good fortune that my landlord had been so obliging. I did not tell them about the scaffolding the year before. I did not say I lived in fear of the day he might decide to sell.

In his 1813 report, Patrick Neill had much to say about landlords' roles in maintaining cottage gardens for their tenants. He found that, in the case of renting from year to year, the tenant 'is often discouraged from meliorating his little spot because of the uncertainty of his tenure, or the dread that his improvements may induce some competitor to bid a few shillings more rent, and thus oust him the following year.' In order to the avoid the resultant neglect of this situation, he strongly recommended 'granting of leases of some years' duration, wherever this is found practicable'. He advised that most kailyards were too small and ought to be enlarged, and that tenants' neglect of their gardens would obviously continue 'as long as cottagers remain till Candlemas [February 2] uncertain whether they are to continue their possession for another season.' Instead, he would have the lease settled at Martinmas (November 11).

MEG BERTERA-BERWICK

The allocation of a house and garden as part of employment, called tied housing, was extremely common for agricultural workers and craftspeople before industrialisation. In addition to the house and kailyard, they might also receive staple grains and fuel in payment for their services. On February 13, 1690, *The Account Book of Sir John Foulis of Ravelston* records that Foulis employed two men as hinds (a married and skilled farm-servant) and in compensation they received, '10 bolls oats and 2 bolls peas, a kowes grass, 6 load of coalls cariage, and a kaill yard, and a house to each of them'.

I wondered if these hinds or their hard-working wives ever despaired at leaving a particular garden. Maybe the garden was such a functional domestic space that it inspired as much affection as a hearth or a window; maybe it was too utilitarian for love. I didn't think I could ever bear to be at the mercy of a particular job in keeping a home or garden; it felt too cruel to consider leaving *everything* when employment changed, and then I remembered that this is how I grew up. Every two to four years, my father's job in the military forced us to leave places we had grown to feel at home in, and every two to four years my mother cried as she undid the garden she had made. Sometimes parts of it could come with us but it didn't matter, because she always made another. It made no sense to me back then, the compulsion to do it all over. This impulse to keep remaking eventual, undeniable heartbreak.

*

Within a month of starting my PhD my body wanted to grow things, as if it was responding to a state of emergency. A colleague told me that it was natural to form an obsession with something unrelated from research for the duration; for her, it had been Mount Everest and its nineteenth-century climbers. I brought seeds and young plants back to my studio flat without really knowing what to do with them, without ever really looking into how to keep them alive, like a beaver trying to make a dam from soft toys and household furnishings. I mourned a fig that wasn't dead, just hibernating; I propagated a grocery store celery that lived weakly for two years. In Inverness, I hid pots full of tomatoes and garlic in a long straight line in the drainage strip behind our cottage flat. I spat with anger when the careless landscapers swept their strimmers too close, gouging holes in my thin plastic containers; there could never be any justice, because the letting agency had been clear that I could keep pots on the front path only, and they could not interfere with the sterile square of green grass that the landscapers mowed erratically. As the bleak disenchantment with academia made it harder to see the point of my life, the compulsion to grow things ate my heart out. I did not know how to justify to myself the longing for land that lived in me like an animal.

In his essay 'Why We Need Gardens', neurologist and naturalist Oliver Sacks coined the term 'hortophilia', the desire to interact with, manage, and tend nature, a cousin to naturalist Edward O. Wilson's theory of biophilia, the love of nature and living things. Sacks described the many patients he had seen improved through time spent in hospital gardens, and the neurodivergent and chronically ill friends who shed their tics and tremors when in natural space. He described dementia and Alzheimer's patients who had forgotten how to tie their shoes or cook a meal, but who knew exactly how to plant the seedlings in the flower bed before them. In his experience, the only two non-pharmaceutical therapies helpful for patients with chronic neurological conditions were music and gardens.

As I came in the front door from every session in the garden, I rushed to my desk to write it all down: the compost I'd spread, seedlings taken out of the cold frame, slugs pulled off the strawberries, contentment evident in the lettuce leaves. I wouldn't have remembered otherwise. The thoughts I had when gardening were as brittle and fleeting as dreams. They would have floated away without leaving any impression on the soft matter of my brain unless I herded them into a clump and pinned them down. The garden grew a shadow life in Word documents and the photo archive. I consulted my journal again and again to remember what was sown when, which was eaten first. I sat with the pictures in the hours after I took them, only able to really *see* the garden then, when I wasn't pretending to look busy to avoid conversation or listening hypervigilantly for the voice of my eccentric neighbour on her chaotic walkabouts.

By now, in the third year, there was a long record to revisit, years to compare. Impossible not to notice, in the rereading, how writing the garden had become an extension of writing myself; a way of keeping track, of reading myself back to me in the future so I knew not to judge myself, or the garden, too harshly. The garden was its own record too; the ground held the shape of my decisions and the heft of my homemade compost, full of our own DNA. I held the garden in nudging marginalia (sow nasturtium, pick parsley), in the crevices under my nails. There was something about this collaborative ground-memory that felt suspiciously intuitive, as if it was inherent, genetic, won off the back of thousands of years of evolution. The longing for land that had lodged itself with a physical ache in my ribs softened and tensed in waves, soothed in the air of the garden, taut in the world outside it.

Sacks did not know exactly how hortophilia worked, though he expressed a general certainty that relationship with nature caused deep changes in brain physiology, hypothesising such relationship may also affect brain structure. In the media, journalists relayed anecdotes about the mental and physical benefits of access to green space with a tone of surprise. Gardening was described as a trend amongst millennials, whose obsession with houseplants was considered almost inexplicable. Findings about health and wellbeing were padded with lukewarm objections to the ways capitalism had commodified land access. The same kind of article repeated with inane regularity. There was nothing in them that reflected the longing and the fear, the wild compulsion. They stacked up like a near-silent pulse, signalling over and over: hortophilia amongst the young and landless needs justification, justification, justification. The love is innate, is innate, is innate, but will not be protected.

On his way to nearby Pollokshaws in *Rambles*, Hugh MacDonald first went through Strathbungo and Crossmyloof, where he met those villages' 'celebrated growers of tulips, pansies, dahlias, and other floricultural favourites'. MacDonald was 'fairly astounded at the multifarious charms which they could discover and point out, in what seemed to our obtuse visual organs a simple tulip or pansy.' It irritated me when he concluded, 'There is something very creditable to such individuals in their enthusiastic love of flowers. We know not, indeed, how a working man could spend his leisure hours more harmlessly or pleasantly, than in the cultivation of a little flower-pot.' Even then, a journalist framing this gardening lark as a pastime that is admirable but not necessary. I felt an urge to instruct MacDonald to pass the pen to these gardeners, to tell them to write me in their own words how they felt the urgency and joy of growing, whether it was merely a pastime to them.

*

From my desk, I had a good view of passers-by observing the garden. Encouraged by their certainty of the beans and the basil, I watched adults wonder if the garlic were onions and assume the cosmos were fennel. People sometimes left offerings; in the first spring, a stranger fully screeched his car to a halt in the middle of the street to ask if I would like any tomato plants, because he had grown too many. During lockdown, I came home one day to find a package of biodegradable pots on my wall, no note or explanation. In the early summer of this third year, a man knocked on our door to proffer a book on vegetable growing that he'd been keeping in his car in case he saw me.

Mine was not the only well cared-for garden in the neighbourhood, but it was one of just a few that continued to grow vegetables intensively after the second lockdown. I managed a triangular relationship between gardener and garden, garden and passers-by, and passers-by and gardener. When people offered things to the garden, I was moved that it didn't have anything to do with *me* so much as with their own personal relationship to a place they passed often. Vegetables are so happily recognisable; recognition encourages deeper looking, because between familiar plants are things that might also be food, but that confound in their unfamiliarity. At least once a week, I watched a parent point through the sweet peas to show their children the lettuce and the apples, naming as much as they could all together. I smiled when little faces lit up as they recognised the strawberries and the raspberries. One particularly small person announced with such astonishment, 'A very good gardener must live here.'

Over coffee, my friend, a fellow neighbour in the building, warned me that the other flat owners were discussing potential building works. Much to our dismay, my landlord's company had been chosen for the labour. Dates were being suggested, maybe as soon as the next spring. I puffed myself up: he'll have to give us proper notice this time, I said,

THE KAILYARDS

not like when the scaffolding went up before. My neighbour fed information back to us through the months as the project stuttered and stalled indefinitely, and rain kept coming through the rooves of the top flats. I thought, *I'll try not to worry until the landlord says something.*

*

The 1895 OS town plan of Glasgow shows a Langside very altered from forty years before. The long row of cottages from the 1859 OS map has been halved, the village green built over with a post office and house, the Victoria Infirmary well established in an old arable field, and dozens of villas built in rows along the curve of the hill. Of the twelve or so kailyards that were recorded in 1859, only two, maybe two-and-a-half remain. They retain their little dashed-line paths and a scattering of bushes and trees, but are diminutive compared to the sweeping gardens of the mansions around them. Instead of apples and gooseberries clustered against the main road, cross-hatched shapes of greenhouses dot the landscape, some as big as the villas they're attached to.

The residents of these mansions were owners and investors of forced labour camps in the global south, proprietors and overseers of factories in the city, entrepreneurs of trading companies that brought sugar, oil, and cotton to Europe. The descendants of Langside's agricultural and artisan working classes were pushed into other neighbourhoods, where newly built tenements housed whole families in one or two small rooms apiece. As in other Scottish cities, with no gardens for growing kale and oats, it was easy for industry leaders to entrap workers into a ruinous diet of white bread, jam, and tea. Such an arrangement fuelled the market for goods produced and exploited in colonised regions, while further facilitating the factory work that enabled imperialist violence. At the 1901 Glasgow International Exhibition, kale and the kailyard were already spoken of in the past tense: 'The cole wort or green kail was for long the chief vegetable of Scotland. The "kail yard" was the cottar's garden: and "kale" became the synonym for "Scotch broth".'

The kailyard survived in places where capitalism and the downstream effects of racialised imperialism were slower to corrode old communities: Shetland, principally, and parts of the Highlands. But in most places, everything was forgotten: the methods of cooking, the comfort in eating, the folklore that shaped the year, the words that shaped the place, the particular conversation between human and plant and ground.

A people who had once made so many words, traditions, poems, and art around a beloved

THE KAILYARDS

vegetable gained a reductive reputation for being vegetable-phobic, for frying the daylights out of everything. It was all lost so completely and efficiently that, when kale re-emerged in the 2000s as a so-called superfood, there was no memory or recognition of its past life in Scotland, no effort to reclaim it as a national vegetable. When the kailyards grew again in the first lockdown, no one knew to see them that way, knew to see them as a resurrection of old and embedded tracts.

The last weaver's cottage and its kailyard were demolished in Langside in 1905. I couldn't find anything about the event in the newspaper archives. I wondered how long it had lain vacant beforehand; if a tenant was displaced so the landlord could sell for tenements; if the garden was full of self-seeded kales and nettles; if there was anyone left from the old days to feel sad about the rubble and the churned-up soil and the gap it left in the face of the street. I thought about the thin, desolate line of my mother's mouth as she dug out her plants to distribute to friends; I knew that someone, somewhere, had been devastated by the grief of old apple trees being felled, the generations of calendula and kale paved over. Maybe all the grieving had happened before, when the other cottages preceded it. Maybe all the grieving happened after, when it was much too late.

*

MEG BERTERA-BERWICK

The morning was still blue at the edges, quiet and cool. A dark handful of worm casts clustered near the lettuce bed. The nasturtium leaves were as large as my hand, and their flowers had gone from pure red to variegated oranges and yellows. It was all a November jumble, even richer in its third year than its generous second. I did slow laps, stroking leaves and taking pictures. My kale plants were still in their pots, perched on top of the soil to mark where they would go in for the winter. But they would never go in. This was the garden's last hour of being its crowded, temperamental, good-smelling best, and the task of absorbing its death felt as impossible as putting round pegs in square holes. Everything so insistently, undeniably alive.

We were given one week's notice to destroy the garden before building works would begin. We asked for compromise, for limited access, and were told it was too expensive. When we argued for a rent reduction while works were ongoing, we were told that the garden was never part of the rental agreement, that we didn't pay for it, that we had been allowed in it by the landlord's generosity and that if we dare ask for money, then he might as well ask us for even more money. I told him that the garden was like an extension of my body; he told us that if we didn't do as we were told, we wouldn't get it back.

THE KAILYARDS

Irritated by our resistance, he sent lackeys to destroy it before the week was through. I woke up to the bent metal of my trellises flung in the back garden, and rushed to the front window to protest. A flunky in hi-vis warily called his boss to report. The phone was handed over and my partner bellowed at the landlord down the receiver while I sat on the edge of my chair, cold and mute and shaking.

Generous neighbours helped me to disembowel the raised beds and carry the still-living compost to be stored in IKEA bags at the back of the communal garden. On my hands and knees, I scraped the last good soil from the garden floor, gently putting worms in the bucket, and cried at how even in its death, the garden absorbed me in the tending of it. I yanked the nasturtiums out of the gravel and apologised to every one of them. As I cut the *Verbena bonariensis* down, a single honeybee came out of nowhere and buzzed around my legs in confusion. I asked my neighbour friend to take a picture of me, one last photo together with the garden. My foot is propped possessively on the raised bed I am meant to take out, my hands resting on the shovel like I've just claimed this land for my own. Somehow I am smiling, but only because it is my friend who is caring for me, who has somehow made me laugh just before.

MEG BERTERA-BERWICK

I stacked the raised beds into a kind of bay in the back garden, and another friend helped me to shovel all the compost from the bags into it, distracting me with gossip. I put the cold frame on top, nestled all the herbs inside for protection, and wrapped pots in bubble wrap to keep the frost off. I took a picture at the end; the garden so vastly diminished, hunched under the empty branches of the tall goat willow. After, I cried so hard I thought I would throw up.

At night, I didn't sleep. I felt as though I couldn't find solid ground, couldn't orient where my body or brain was in relation to land. The garden was gone; so where was I? The garden was the shape of the mint between the lettuce and sorrel, was the scent of compost and stone, was the borage seeds sleeping in soil, and now it was all undone, unmoored, unmade. Flat-packed in the back, rogue amputated nasturtium arms still strewn about the front. The garden held so much of my memory; where would I keep it now?

*

In the 1865 *Clydesdale Flora*, botanist Roger Hennedy noted that both colewort and common turnip were found growing freely along the banks of the Rivers Cart, Kelvin, and Clyde, escapees from cultivated fields. He was a friend of Hugh MacDonald, with whom he walked in the places

THE KAILYARDS

around Glasgow, pointing out the vegetation along their route. 'Our flower-loving friend is now in all his glory poking and prying along the vegetable fringe that skirts the path. Every now and then we are startled by his exclamations of delight, as some specimen of more than ordinary beauty meets his gaze'. (MacDonald)

In 1994, a medieval drain of Paisley Abbey was excavated. In the ancient silt of the White Cart Water, archaeobotanist Camilla Dickson found the vestiges of late medieval Renfrewshire gardens: apple pips, fig seeds, blackberry seeds, grains of black oats, splinters of a hybrid wheat-rye, fragments of walnuts, and seeds of both *Brassica rapa* (turnip rape) and *Brassica oleracea* (kale and cabbage), dating to around 1500. For four hundred years or more, the gardens jumped their fences, landing in adjoining fields, hitching a ride downstream in the rivers.

In the spring after it was destroyed, I kept finding my garden in the street, between cracks in the pavement. For a while there was a fully-grown calendula between the footpath and a garden wall, sat next to a withered red-veined sorrel, just as they would have leaned against each other in my beds. I didn't notice the sorrel until after I had taken a picture of the calendula, and then I saw my sorrel everywhere, buddied up to fat crowns of ancient dandelions. I found Sutherland kale growing in the pavement down the road, offspring of a plant that set seed in the garden last year. The pavement-kales quickly flowered, and their offspring popped up across the street from them, and now a third generation of stunted pavement-dwellers were setting seed too. They had meandered all the way down to the White Cart Water, to wedge themselves in the flood wall. I lingered by them when we walked past, would not let the dog pee on them. Like meeting a friend unexpectedly in the street, so joyful. And yet.

I plucked a dry pod rattling with its little ball-bearing seeds, rubbed it open as we walked along. The seeds skittered across the pavement and came to rest in the leaf mould against the flood defence. I wondered how long the kale had seeded itself for after the kailyards had gone, whether it was still along the riverbanks a year or five later. All these gardens I mourned, my own and the old kailyards, suddenly did not feel so dead as I had believed. Here was all my memory scattered smaller and smaller in the neglected margins of the city; here were old shapes of old kailyards still persisting, biding their time till they made it down river, into ground cracked open by the warmth of manure.

EMMA HARDING

WILD TRACK

When you die, I go to the woods. It is late December and the footpaths are deep black mires. I surrender to them, willingly. The effort of wading through thick mud, stumbling over hidden tree roots, freeing myself from brambles, is just the real-world manifestation of what is happening in my head. I am stumbling over the shock of your absence, wading through this new reality of your loss. At least when I'm walking, my heart beats in a less chaotic rhythm. If I could, I'd keep walking and never stop.

Every morning at 2am, I am woken by the same slam of grief, the same flip of a whale's tail against my chest. Every morning, I relearn your death. Then I lie awake in the dark, not-listening to the radio, and once the hours have ticked down, get up, make breakfast for my son, move through the morning as through fog. My lungs are corseted with a pointless panic. The corset tightens and tightens until there comes a point when I'm propelled through the front door.

I go to the woods. I have a subconscious need for wilderness, choose the disorder of the woods rather than sheep-manicured fields, or the wide skies of

WILD TRACK

the local reservoir. Something in me needs the dark of the canopy, needs the tangle, the leaf-mulch, the scutterings in the brush.

I stand in the woods and listen. This act of paying attention slows my breathing, gives me a foothold in clarity. You and I are both creatures of sound. We have spent our lives working in radio, our ears accustomed to sifting the geological layers of the sound-world. Both attuned to the ways in which even the subtlest of noises communicates information, affects emotion, mood.

If I were standing here with a microphone, I'd be recording wild track, a technical term for recording ambient sound. But to me it's a coining that's always suggested something more thrillingly metaphorical – sound gone wild, gone rogue.

Whenever I record wild track, there's the moment when I hit the red button and world dawns in my headphones, extravagant, hyper-real. I can hear everything in front of me in sharp, insect-feet-on-bark detail, as well as everything behind, above, far distant. We cannot visualise four dimensions, but perhaps we can hear them. And even standing here without a microphone, my ears are trained to attentiveness, a sensation captured by the poet Alice Oswald in her poem 'Woods etc', where she describes the experience of walking into 'increasing' woods with *hearing like a widening wound*.

And now I stand in the increasing woods and listen, my ears pulling apart the different threads in the weave of sound. There are the birds of course. Though it seems there are fewer birds than there ought to be. Is that the normal muting of winter, or a sign of ecological depletion? Still, I can pick out dunnocks in the hedgerow, coal tits, long-tailed tits, blackbird, robin, thrush, gossipy starlings gathering in a distant tree, the distant alarum of pheasant. There are rustlings in the undergrowth too. The sudden starts of squirrels, breaking cover, the cautious concentrated foraging of smaller mammals. And then there is the creak from within the trees themselves, like the laboured breathing of an elderly man.

As I walk, twigs snap beneath my feet, a bramble catches on my trouser leg and, pulling free, I hear the bush shudder back into itself. And from the crack and rustle, fragments of poetry float up, lines with strong iambic feet that match my own footfall. *'I leant upon a coppice gate/When frost was spectre grey.' 'Though worlds of wanwood leafmeal lie'.* I say out loud as much as I remember, then have to pull out my phone in frustration and google the rest.

A new sound now. I stop. I stand in the woods and listen. After weeks of rain, the thin woodland stream has burst its banks and flows urgently downhill, as if desperate to empty its load, as if it knows it has overreached the borders of itself.

WILD TRACK

I am not used to being so out of control of my emotions. Colleagues and friends often remark on my calm unflappability in the face of pressure. So much so that I have come to believe this is a defining part of my persona. But it is dangerous, perhaps, to buy into the myths others create for you.

I go to the woods to let my calm go rogue, cut loose, flap wild.

You are too young when your body suddenly succumbs to disease. In August, you are bemusedly showing me your swollen legs, in September you are diagnosed with a serious illness. I trawl the internet, try to decipher medical research papers and articles in *The Lancet*. These present me with statistics I choose not to believe. After all, I'm no expert.

It is autumn 2020. You are in and out of hospital, but no one can visit you there due to Covid restrictions. But we speak every day. I send you daft jokes, gifs of kangaroos. And when you're released from hospital, I call round with groceries, cook dinner, watch old movies with you. You say you keep imagining what it would be like to wear 'a well suit' and together we conjure ever wilder possibilities for what that suit would look like.

In early December, you reluctantly submit to hospital once more. We still talk every day, but your voice is increasingly thin, your texts sparser, more confused. One morning, I call you for a chat. You manage to say hello and then I hear the nurse helping to manoeuvre you out of bed. Perhaps the phone is lying on your sheets at this point. Everything is happening at a distance. I hear the nurse say, 'I'm worried about you.' You say, 'No need to worry about me.' She says, 'But I do worry.' And then I hear you groan in pain. There is some kind of struggle to stand, to move. The nurse trying to steady you. I can hear your laboured breathing. More groaning. I clutch the phone, hoping that it will all be all right in a moment, that you'll be back on the line with a self-mocking quip. But the groaning doesn't stop. And then someone turns off the phone. That is the last time I hear your voice.

The following day, I learn you're in intensive care, diagnosed with Covid. This is December 2020, a month before any vaccines will become available. You spend your final week unconscious on a ventilator. You always hated Christmas, and just to prove it, you die late on Christmas night, a nurse holding your hand. Your traumatised sister can only watch on Facetime as your body gives up.

I am shocked by the physicality of grief, by the sensation that the fibres of my heart are being slowly ripped apart. How crazily literal heartbreak is.

I went out to the hazel wood/Because a fire was in my head. That day I go to the woods. I go to the woods the next day, and the next. I am not seeking

WILD TRACK

the consolation of nature, or the peace of wild things, I seek confrontation with what is raw and wild and uncontainable in me. I need the tumult of the woods, the unpredictability of their music – *the uproar gathering high* of John Clare's oaks, Sylvia Plath's rooks that *croak havoc*, Gerard Manley Hopkins' ash-boughs that tabour on the heavens.

It's a commonplace to say that Western culture is woefully inadequate at discussing death, so that when we are faced with it, as we all must be, we are taken by surprise. Intellectually, we know we are mortal – on our GCSE English Literature paper, we carefully circled all the metaphors of time and rot in a Metaphysical poem, opined loftily on Elizabethan attitudes to death. We spend hours of our lives watching news reports and TV dramas that remind us of the everydayness of loss, the fragility of the human body. But the first time we lose someone significant, we feel utter disbelief that the universe could treat us so shoddily. How can this be happening to me? We are ill-prepared for the wilderness of grief, its lack of structure.

In Malory's *Le Morte D'Arthur*, Tristram disappears into the woods, tears off his clothes and succumbs to a wild madness rooted in his despairing love for La Beale Isoud – *and then Sir Tristram would go into the wilderness, and brast down the trees and boughs.* Brast is a Middle English word meaning 'burst', but here the nearness of 'brast' to 'breast' makes us feel that Tristram himself is the one who is bursting open. His madness is dangerous, entirely at odds with the strictly codified society he belongs to. Knights are meant to be fully in control of themselves, models of courage and endurance. And yet, and yet…we can't help but feel that Malory's sympathy is with Tristram.

You loved the Arthurian stories. Growing up, your older sister had read to you from Roger Lancelyn Green and included you in her games of knights and maidens, dressing you up in a cardboard breastplate, knighting you with a sword. You once told me that Tristram was your favourite knight and if I asked you why – surely I did? – I don't remember your answer. This bothers me now. I hoard memories of you desperately – your texts, your anecdotes, your favoured phrases, postcards of your favourite paintings, every clue to yourself that you ever gave me. I construct a playlist of music you loved, then find I cannot listen to it. But what was it about Tristram? I am furious with my memory's limitations. My head's on fire. My breast is brast.

The flight into the wild wood is a common notion in cultures around the world. It is true of Merlin, of Enkidu in the Epic of Gilgamesh, of Buddha, of Sweeney. But Irish folklore also offers us a wild woman of the woods, Mis, who is so grief-stricken by the death of her warrior father, Daire Dhoidgheal, that she is transformed into a bird-like creature and flies to the mountains. Here, she lives in the forest, her skin sprouting fur and feathers, her nails lengthening to talons. With her bare hands she rips apart any animals or humans who come near. Her retreat from civilisation, her falling apart, are a logical response to grief.

I was about to write 'I too feel deranged by grief.' But that's not right. That's not it at all. In fact, I feel extraordinary clarity. I know all I have lost. And because I am alone in the woods, I can give it voice. I can brace myself against a beech trunk and howl, send my own wild-track into the canopy of trees.

But my own transformations are temporary. In a couple of hours, I'll have to reassume human form, stand in the kitchen chopping vegetables for dinner, answer an urgent work email, reassure my parents that I'm okay. *I'm okay.*

Society gives grief structure through the rituals of mourning, the social gatherings, the public memorials. These rituals are important, necessary. But grief also needs to be able to cut loose, to forage in the undergrowth, to be alone with itself. Although I weep with gratitude for the kindness of friends, grief, I am discovering, is an entirely solitary experience. It is the specific love of one person for another.

I am offered counselling, helplines, bereavement

chatrooms. Some of these I will use. But I am already aware that my grief is not something to be solved or managed. It is my animal-self. It is all instinct. It is perhaps the most truthful state I have ever known. More truthful than love? Perhaps. Because this is love with no audience, no object, other than a lost invisible one, who can no longer be charmed or hurt.

I stand in the woods and listen. The trochees of great-tits. White flashes of breast feather like fireflies among the dark twigs.

In reality, there is no true wilderness in this corner of England. I live in Kent which, for all its varied beauty, is mostly managed beauty. But it has been this way for centuries – much of the woodland I walk through would once have been part of a royal deer chase, given by William the Conqueror to the de Clare family, passing through hands as various as Edward II's lover, Piers Gaveston, and Frances Walsingham, daughter of Elizabeth I's spymaster and widow of poet Philip Sidney. A place of pleasure, as well as a valuable source of timber, venison, rabbits, iron.

But these woods were here before the Normans. The Weald of Kent – the world 'weald' is related to the German 'wald' – was known by the Romans and the Saxons for its impenetrable forests, so my woodland of oak, beech and birch feels like the nearest thing to an ancient Kentish wilderness. And it remains the most wooded part of England, with small woods connected to one another by gills (or valleys), sunken lanes, shaws and ancient hedge banks. From the air, these wooded highways create a patchwork effect, but they're also important wildlife corridors, enabling creatures to move around to breed and forage. The gills of the Weald, with their streams and damp ravines, are home to unique mosses and liverworts, and to plants with redolent names such as the hay-scented buckler-fern or coral-root bittercress.

Today, the preservation and expansion of woodland – the most complex of the UK's terrestrial habitats – is once more at the heart of the environmental agenda. Three quarters of the woodland in the High Weald is deemed to be 'ancient', defined as having existed continuously since at least 1600. This is rare and precious. Only 2.5 per cent of the UK is covered by ancient woodlands, but many threatened species of insects, birds and mammals depend on them. Their biodiversity is the result of hundreds of years of continuity, which means there's no way of replacing or emulating it. Once it's lost, it's lost forever.

Our impending ecological disaster sometimes made you weep. In the early weeks of the first Covid lockdown, the forests of your native Australia were burning and your sorrow was deep and visceral. You wanted to translate your grief into action, said you planned to join Extinction Rebellion, suggested we both sign up for a tree-planting initiative once lockdown was over. But then you got sick.

I stand in the woods and listen. A single magpie lands on a branch above me. I don't expect to see a second, don't bother to look.

Woods contain turning points, moments of decision or epiphany. Frost's road not taken. Dante's mid-life crisis in the dark, savage wood – *selva selvaggia e aspra e forte*. Yeats's wandering Aengus goes out to the hazel wood because a fire is in his head and leaves the ordinary world behind. He fishes a silver trout from a stream and it turns into a glimmering girl. She is the creature of a moment, but he spends the rest of his life looking for her. *I will find out where she is gone.* We know his mission to be futile, we recognise his obsession, while luxuriating in the beauty of its golden and silver apples. But we don't learn from it. I walk through the woods knowing that, on some level, I am looking for you.

You are nowhere. And these woods are the closest I can get to nowhere.

I stand in the woods and listen. Aware of my inarticulacy in the face of nature's eloquence, the gaps in our human understanding. Like Hardy's darkling thrush whose evensong seems to contains *some blessed hope whereof he knew/And I was unaware.*

WILD TRACK

Elizabeth Jennings' poem 'Into the Hour' marks a moment of transition when the speaker finds a new way of living with the wilderness that comes with a loved one's death. One spring, the speaker is surprised to discover that she is once more able to take pleasure in the changing seasons, in the apple-blossom on the bough. This symbol of continuance no longer represents loss, but Paradise here on earth, a Paradise into which the love for the lost person can be folded. A love that *has no considered end*.

I stand in the woods and listen. A sudden gust of wind plays the leafless branches above me. *This roaring peace*, as Edward Thomas wrote. These trees are decades older than me, than you. Their lives contain generations of human deaths. And now your death is written into this year's rings, just beneath the bark, a grave-marker in every trunk. One day too, the year of my death will be printed into them. And I am glad of this anonymous memorial.

I stand in the woods and listen. And I hear impossible things: leaves rotting, worms moving through dark soil, tree roots uncurling beneath my feet, the slow certain upward push of bluebell shoots. Things about to emerge. The life coiled into the leaf bud. The cusp of hope. Love with no considered end.

But I am not out of the woods yet.

DAVID HIGGINS

MINIBEASTS

'Who would like to hold him?'

To my surprise, each kid puts a hand up and shouts 'Me!'

I am less enthusiastic about interacting with this alien creature. Its segmented, tubular body is as long as my forearm and shines in the midday sun like polished obsidian. The legs are tiny, more like frills than limbs, and there are too many to count. They writhe and wriggle. E— steps forward, grinning, and holds out his hand.

'What does it feel like?'

'Tickly!'

The other kids take their turn and then a few of the adults, including me. The millipede wraps itself around my wrist. Its legs are softer than I had expected, not scratchy, and reassuringly dry. I don't fancy holding the African land snail. But all the children do, wiping their hands on the grass afterwards. They also love the cockroaches and leaf insects. E— crouches down and stares intently at the orange-black tarantula.

'Can I hold it?'

'I'm afraid not,' says Rob, the custodian of exotic

MINIBEASTS

minibeasts. 'Males can be aggressive, and he doesn't like being handled. He might bite.'

I think E— would happily take the risk. But we content ourselves with watching the spider trying to escape from his plastic container.

Rob is one of many local contacts whom my mother has marshalled in the organisation of her eightieth birthday party, held at a village hall in Bedfordshire. Mum is modest, self-sacrificing, and has never had a party like this before. Despite various setbacks, including fracturing her wrist three weeks beforehand, she has succeeded in making it happen. I give a welcoming speech to the guests and enjoy the cheap laughs elicited by a joke about her organising it single-handedly. (Two weeks later, the joke is on me when I go out at dusk to look for nightjars, trip over a tree root, and break my own wrist.)

After the minibeasts are packed away, an impromptu game of cricket starts up on the small meadow outside the hall. To my surprise, E— joins in. He has never played before and is outclassed by kids who go to the kind of school where the sport is mandatory. He enjoys himself, though. He's only six, but strong and well-coordinated. Occasionally, I shout over to remind him that he needs to face the ball with the flat side of the bat. One of the other dads helps him to take the correct stance. I wonder if, like me, E— finds large social occasions difficult.

Later, when he seems tired, I plonk him in a quiet corner of the hall and let him watch YouTube on my tablet.

During the cricket, I talk to an uncle whom I haven't seen for a decade. He's still a big man but saddened and diminished by age. Voice quieter, beard white, skin turning translucent, as if he already has one foot in the next world. He uses crutches and rests his bulk on the bonnet of his brother-in-law's van.

'You should come and visit me in Montreal,' he says.

'I'd love to. Haven't dared take the kids on a plane yet. But maybe soon.'

He's been asking me to visit for thirty years, and I never have. As we talk, I keep my eye on my little daughter. She oscillates between chasing a friendly dog, disrupting the game of cricket, climbing into the boot of our car, and demanding chocolate.

Swallows flit low across the field next door. High above it, skylarks sing, their rapid trilling tempered by gentle variations of pitch. I imagine the notes modulating as the birds move up and down in the air. Without my binoculars, though, I can't pick them out. Somewhere in the distance, a greenfinch lets out a pained wheeze, as if he has mislaid his steroid inhaler. When E— was younger, I'd have pointed out these things to him. Now I don't bother. Birds are too distant, elusive: he prefers the intimacy of bugs.

*

After the party, we pack up undrunk wine and uneaten food and drive back to Mum's: a nondescript four-bedroom house in an unpretentious village. For a long time, I thought it was unbelievably boring. Now I'd be happy to move from the city, if it was practical, and live there myself: fieldfares and redwings in the winter; swallows and yellow wagtails in the summer; rooks and house sparrows all year round.

It's the first warm evening of the year. I want to get out, preferably on my own. I'm tired from socialising and kid-wrangling. My uncle looms heavy in my mind. I'm tempted to sneak away, but I ask if anyone wants to join me. Eventually, I leave with my brother, sister, and E—. As an incentive, I tell him there might be some bugs or even a green woodpecker. He has seen the latter in photos and admires their long, ant-seeking tongues.

Once we leave together, I'm glad. E— hardly ever sees my siblings. And it's always good to get him away from the TV. At the village bus stop, we climb over a collapsing stile into a meadow of long grass and tall buttercups, enclosed by hawthorn hedgerows covered in bright blossom and hoverflies. We drink in rich greens and yellows, with smatterings of white, overlooked by a purplish sky. The air is heavy and sickly. Rooks perch in silhouette on a distant power line. My son runs off the path, shouting and laughing. But excitement soon turns into something else. He screams, and rushes forward to join my brother and sister, who have walked ahead. I catch up.

'What's the matter?'

'Crane flies!!'

Perhaps he's just playing. But then a crane fly floats between us. He screams again, flinches, lashes out, as if he has lost control of his body. I kneel, cuddle him, speak consoling words. *Crane flies can't hurt you. They're good for birds and animals. You're brave. You love creepy crawlies. I love you.* My head close to his, I have a different perspective. The grass stalks and flowers are buzzing with life. Crane flies loom at my eye level, veering unpredictably, their legs dangling.

We're at the top edge of the meadow, next to a wheat field. I make the decision to keep going. (I wonder now whether this was to protect E— from walking back through the long grass, or because I was doing a terrible dad thing of sticking to a bad plan.) Crane flies don't seem fond of wheat, but now every aerial creature is threatening. With my brother's help, and ignoring my creaking ankle joints, I get E— on to my shoulders. I hold on tight to his legs as he twists and judders. My siblings form a phalanx guarding us on either side. They try to distract by asking about toys, hobbies, school. A large and spindly crane fly heads at us, colliding with my sunglasses. It's hard to keep hold of my son, or my temper, as he screams and struggles and smacks me hard on the head.

When a couple of yellow wagtails pop up from the green stalks, I recall, as if peering a long way back in time, that finding them had been my main aim for the walk. We risk going off the footpath to get home quicker and march precariously across crumbly clay to the road through the village. A convertible accelerates past, ignoring the speed limit. I recoil at the noise of its engine. The middle-aged driver – and this may be a retrospective flourish – has a smug look on his face. I picture a tractor pulling out in front of him, leading to a decapitation. We near Mum's house. E— flinches and cries out at a wood pigeon clumsily departing from an oak tree's canopy.

I blame myself for not considering how wired E— had been from the party. But, at bedtime, and entirely uncharacteristically, he says, 'Thank you for looking after me.'

*

It's a rough night. I'm in the process of coming off the antidepressants that I've been taking for five years. They've helped me through dark times, but have marked my body, leading to weight gain and possibly the beginnings of liver disease. Insomnia is the worst of the withdrawal symptoms, made worse by the resurgence of old allergies. Lying in the dark, I feel stuffed up, uncomfortable, beset by buzzing, whirring anxieties. I think about Dad. He hated the nights, too. He medicated himself with booze; I've used mirtazapine. Not so different.

We have two rooms between four of us, so I'm sharing a double bed with my daughter. Despite her small size, she takes up a lot of space. She wriggles, snores, coughs. Twice she wakes and complains angrily that I'm not her mum.

Around three thirty, I get up. I'm groggy, troubled. But I'm not trapped. A couple of weeks earlier, I heard of a place just a short drive away from Mum's village. I hardly dare believe that it exists. I'm not even sure how to access it, but I've checked an Ordnance Survey map and found a possible starting point.

I leave the house just as the day emerges and drive slowly along the empty road, keeping watch for barn owls quartering the arable fields. There's a flutter in my stomach: the excitement of leaving behind, however briefly, the normal responsibilities of work and family. Movement on the tarmac ahead turns out to be a small group of yellowhammers, their heads sun-bright in my headlights. They seem reluctant to fly off, so I drive around them. Flattening a red-listed species would not be an auspicious start to the day.

After passing through a village, I turn up a narrow lane that looks like a private road. A couple of shadowy shapes fly into a copse. Tawny owls? I stop to peruse one of those complicated signs that landowners erect when they want to keep people away but have no legal basis for doing so, before driving on past an ugly building, crowned by garish letters spelling T-A-R-G-E-T-S-H-O-O-T-I-N-G. So far, so unpromising. But I find the footpath sign and park up.

My heart is beating too quickly, too loudly. Too much caffeine; too little sleep. I pause for a minute, taking deep breaths in through my nostrils and out through my mouth. When I feel calm enough, I step out of the car.

The path leads into a dim strip of woodland, with the shooting range on one side. I listen intently as I walk. A harsh bark startles me. *Just a muntjac*, I reassure myself. A blackcap jangles, improvises. It's beautiful, but not what I'm here for. Then, just a few yards further in, I've found it. Louder than I'd expected, unpredictable, ever surprising: sometimes liquid, sinuous; sometimes mechanical, staccato. I stand and listen. I wonder if I've ever before listened with such concentration. Not that I have any choice in the matter: the song demands it.

Many authors have tried to describe the nightingale's magic. This is John Clare in 'The Progress of Rhyme':

> 'Chew-chew chew-chew,' and higher still:
> 'Cheer-cheer cheer-cheer,' more loud and shrill:
> 'Cheer-up cheer-up cheer-up,' and dropt
> Low : 'tweet tweet jug jug jug,' and stopt
> [...]
> 'Wew-wew wew-wew, chur-chur chur-chur,
> Woo-it woo-it': could this be her?
> 'Tee-rew tee-rew tee-rew tee-rew,
> Chew-rit chew-rit,' and ever new,
> 'Will-will will-will, grig-grig grig-grig.'

Clare is one of my favourite writers, but the more he tries to describe the nightingale's song, the more glaring the gap between the description and the original. He understood as well as anyone that writing could never match real encounters with the more-than-human. But he also understood the importance of trying to represent the unrepresentable: an act of connection, solidarity, intimacy.

MINIBEASTS

Nightingales are birds, like bitterns and nightjars, whose sounds are unmistakable but who are very hard to see. Their elusiveness has long made them objects of fable and fascination. Clare follows the literary convention of representing the nightingale as female, but it's the males who sing. I don't want to disturb this one, although I'm desperate to see him. Tentatively, I try to get closer and immediately scratch my hand on a spiky hawthorn branch. Taking this as a warning, I retreat.

Further on, the path widens as it enters an area that is more scrub than woodland. Beautifully flowering hawthorn and blackthorn stand dense and deep on either side of me. I am enveloped in song: chiffchaffs, garden and willow warblers, blackcaps, common and lesser whitethroats – and nightingales. Earlier this year, I failed to find even one at a previously reliable site. I wonder if they have all come here: sometimes I can hear two or three at the same time.

I soon realise that, in this rich landscape, I must rely on my ears and not my eyes. In fact, that morning, I don't see many birds at all. Most are buried deep within the scrub.

An open area appears to my right. Di-di-di-di-di-di-di-di-di-di-di-di-di-di-di-di… Grasshopper warblers trilling loudly: the first I've heard this year. Two, no three. Invisible. I hear a sudden 'cuck-ooo' from further away, but foliage obscures my view. A nightingale starts singing right next to the path. I spend five, ten minutes trying to pick it out. No chance.

At a field edge, I see linnets and yellowhammers, before turning round with the aim of walking slowly back to the car. A man and woman approach from the opposite direction. It's still early; I feel unreasonably offended by having my solitude disturbed. The pair are surveying for the local wildlife trust, which has just purchased the site from a visionary farmer who had let it rewild. We whisper. I rhapsodise. They're friendly but focused on their task, so we don't speak for long. Just after they leave, a small but robust bird alights silently at the top of a hawthorn bush. I assume a robin, but still check in my binoculars. The breast is pale, rather than red, the wings are rusty brown, the tail is broad, and the eyes are large and black. A nightingale.

Just before I move on, I hear a softly undulating call from behind me. I walk for a bit, then stop and turn back. Surely it isn't? I reach the surveyors.

'Did I just hear a turtle dove?'

The man puts his fingers to his lips. 'We just saw a pair of them fly off,' he whispers, while pointing ahead along the path.

'We'd appreciate if you didn't tell anyone.' The woman is even quieter than the man. 'We're trying to keep it a secret, until the end of breeding season.'

'Sure: no problem.'

They walk off. I'd like to follow, in the hope of stumbling across the turtle doves. But I should get back. It's warming up now. Insects emerge, including a few crane flies. The dawn chorus shows no sign of abating. I walk in the direction of the car.

'Cuck-ooo,' this time, much closer.

I scan the sky and glimpse, briefly above the hawthorns, two cuckoos chasing each other with hawk-like agility. A courting pair, I assume. I've never seen that before.

Nightingales and turtle doves are in steep decline in the UK, with both species losing more than 90 per cent of their numbers in the last fifty years. They're increasingly confined to a small number of sites. Cuckoos are more widespread, but their numbers have dropped by around three quarters in the same period. It's likely, too, that taking 1970 as a baseline – while sensible given the available data – obscures serious declines before then. In the last few years, I've learned a lot about Britain's bird life; in the process, I've become intimately acquainted with loss.

Reconnecting with the natural world in middle age has made my life richer, more colourful, more meaningful. It's lightened the heaviness of existence. However, as I get older, I feel the fragility of our lives with ever-increasing intensity. And this feeling has become entangled with my horror at the winnowing away of once common wildlife, and our disconnection from the rhythms of nature. The prospect of my own death, and the deaths of my loved ones, might be more bearable if it seemed like life in all its beauty would carry on when we are gone.

But the future offered by late capitalism often looks grey and denuded. I wonder what room our obsession with economic growth and shiny trivialities leaves for nightingales, just as I fear what it's doing to our children, beset as they are by enticements to stay indoors and consume rather than engaging with the outside world. This is not a problem that can be solved at an individual level: perhaps not even collectively. But one response is to cherish places of hope and the power of unexpected encounters. This morning has reminded me that alternative futures are possible.

*

A couple of days later, and back home in the north, I prise E— from the TV and march him to the local playing field to play frisbee. He finds screens calming and compulsive. Getting him outside can be a battle. On this occasion, he is particularly reluctant, so I bribe him with an ice cream.

MINIBEASTS

We are both nervous, knowing that crane flies tend to come out in the evenings. I assure him, probably inaccurately, that they mostly hang around near farms rather than people's houses.

As we walk up the ginnel through the estate, we discuss what we've learned about them. *Lots of different species. Sometimes called daddy longlegs. Only live for a few days. Not venomous and don't bite. Some don't even eat. Their legs help to stabilise them and to sense dangers.* I try to explain why insects matter, and that there aren't as many as there used to be, and that we should be pleased if we see lots of them. Often, my son is. He looks under rocks for woodlice; catches grasshoppers on our overgrown lawn. But, when it comes to crane flies, I suspect he'd prefer it if the whole country were mowed and pesticided.

Through a narrow strip of woodland, there are midges, whiteflies, a darting butterfly that might be a meadow brown. E— is jumpy and zooms past the long grass at the edge of the playing field. I'm relieved to see that the rest of it has been recently cut short.

My son throws hard, fast, and accurately. But he wants to try for longer and longer distances, making it difficult for us to direct and catch the frisbee. One of my throws hits him in the face. He cries, shouts, blames me. I fear an excursion will once again end in chaos. But I apologise, hug him, and we return to the game.

A couple of small dogs wander over. One is a dark, sausagey beast and the other a pale terrier type. I tense up. These dogs are not barking or rushing, however: just interested. A tracksuited woman in late middle age, jogging behind them, shouts out 'they're friendly!'

The dark one peels off and the pale one trots over to E—. He jumps up, in a gentle way, and then sits quietly between my son's legs. The woman comes over and tells us that she has been visiting a sick friend down the road and that she doesn't normally take the dogs out at this time and that the dark dachshund loves other dogs but that this dog loves children and that she was thinking of contacting Leeds General Infirmary to see if he could visit the children's ward there. E— strokes the dog; the dog appears delighted. I can't explain how I know – perhaps a subtle change in how he stands – but it's clear that my son's anxiety has melted away.

On the walk home, we talk about how animals can help sick people feel better. I tell him that if you are ill and can see trees and plants then that can help you recover more quickly. And how sometimes people need treatment for their bodies and sometimes for their minds.

'So if you're really scared of something you can see a doctor?'

MINIBEASTS

'Yes. There are doctors called psychiatrists. And there are people called counsellors or therapists.'

'Do they talk to children?'

'Some do. But you need special training. It's different from talking to adults.'

'They must be very nice people.' A thoughtful pause. 'I hope we see that dog again. Do you think he will go to the hospital?'

'Maybe. There might be rules. But I hope so.'

We are back in the ginnel. Delicately pink flowers and green, palmate leaves emerge tentatively through cracks in the concrete. My phone informs me that the plant is probably herb Robert. I repeat the name under my breath several times, trying to lodge it in my memory.

E—, who often talks continuously, has been quiet for a minute or two. I offer him my hand; he clutches it. I wonder how old he will be when holding hands with me starts to seem silly.

'Can you talk to therapists about anything?'

'Yes. And they're not allowed to tell anyone what you said. It's between you and them.' 'Could you talk about being scared of crane flies, or of your family dying?'

'Yes,' I say. 'Yes. Things like that.'

NEHA SINHA

IBIS SEA

The Covid-19 pandemic was like a sea that swept us up and spat us out on little bars of sand. I was under water a lot of the time, suspended in stupor, surrounded by unrecognisable detritus. The sea was around me, but also inside me: my lungs and head, and occasionally my heart, felt constantly touched by dirty water. When the disease let me go, the chains of the lockdown were still around us – large, amorphous, each day melding into the other: another vast sea that moved of its own accord.

In the first throes of the lockdown in 2020, though, a scent of adventure was in the air. Could I test the chains in my cage – the depth of the sea – just a little? Could I take a longer route while stockpiling groceries and medicines? Spring 2020 had come as it always does, days golden and bracing, with native trees becoming torches of light. The Semal tree, the *Bombax ceiba*, began offering its red and orange flowers to the world. The tree was tall and imposing, with a perfect branching formation: an open umbrella, some called it.

That spring, I saw the first red Semal flowers of the year from my terrace. The bottom of the sky was touched with large, waxy blossoms that had opened in a sudden, ridiculously rich profusion. A Common myna came to inspect the bounty, hopping from flower to branch in its brown tuxedo. Parakeets arrived, screeching and wheeling through the sky, missiles that launched themselves at the flowers – no investigations, just assault. I couldn't see it from my terrace, but I knew the ground must be thickly carpeted by the flowers that were inspected, half-eaten, and casually flung on to the earth in the free manner that birds have.

The flowering trees were calling me. They were going to be my lighthouses across the sea. I had to be near enough to feel them, if not touch them. I got into my red car, which, happily, matched the flowers. I'd steal satisfaction through the pandemic, I told myself with some urgency. I would find flowers and adventure, the best places. I charted the trees I could see through a longish, circuitous grocery drive – a Semal on a road divider, one in a colony park, and one next to a booze shop. Each tree had flowers that were two to three storeys up, some shaking with gentle laughter – the movements of birds, bees and squirrels in the blossoms. I made mental notes of the birds I saw: garden birds like Indian white eyes and purple sunbirds, forest birds like grey hornbills that pecked at the buds, everything looking giddy with nectar and floral proximity.

Too soon, my morning ended and it was time to go home – to merge into the sameness of each day, to sink into the pandemic prison. But then, I saw something. A huge red blaze, placed against the sky. Like the bouquet of a firecracker, seen only at times of celebration. Tall enough to be visible over a flyover, with a sort of lofty, above-it-all feeling. There had to be more than one Semal tree, because could a single tree be such a huge lighthouse?

It seemed to me the car's steering wheel turned by itself, the machine and I one in our determination to find out. It was like acting on the childhood impulses of bringing puppies, kittens and sandy shells home. I heard my mother's gentle voice, threaded with a seam of iron: 'When you do these things, I'm left to clean up. You go to school.' But there was no school now, and I was an adult. I was bending lockdown rules only slightly. We were meant to be out just for essential needs, and my essential need of seeing this once-in-a-year sight burned in my chest, powering my determination.

When I tried, I saw that three Semal trees had joined hands to form the lighthouse over the lockdown sea. It was gloriously red and raw. It tasted of freedom, the kind of soaring poem you sing when something is born. That freedom was partly because of the atavistic sight of masses of flowers, sitting atop spiny trunks. Another part was the thrilling feeling of having snatched something from the pandemic. The blossoms themselves were raw and stirring, not graceful puffs. They were how a child would imagine flowers to be if she was given a thick, red crayon. A bold thing, a gloriously obvious thing, made roughly, with sticky, candy-stained fingers. No delicate lines, but an electrifying force of being that leapt from the page. Five large petals. A cup-shaped centre. Stamens and stigma that seemed to be pulsing, spilling out of the flower like ferns reaching for the light. A bloom full of nectar, so brimful that even fallen flowers would have clear ambrosia in them. This was the drink of choice for every wild creature that could stop by. I wanted to place my face forward, and drink in the sight through the pores of my skin. I was in my place: watching energy and beauty and life in a lighthouse that had grown itself.

I'd seen flying fox bats, hornbills, sunbirds, parakeets, starlings, barbets and squirrels feeding on Semal nectar before.

That day, I spied something else.

I had first spotted them in imitation Egyptian papyrus. And then, in wild places, doing ferocious things. Near wetlands, stabbing soggy ground with their long, wicked beaks. Fixing their pitiless gaze on prey, and then wrestling with snakes, and swallowing frogs whole. Extracting an entire trinket snake from the grounds of a genteel garden in Delhi, bringing a sense of wilfulness their manicured surroundings could not tame. They were like fairy tales brought to life – odd, beautiful, but with a decided hint of menace. Even the young ones looked infinitely old, here from another age. A kind of mythical being which was like a bird, but also like a scaly-necked reptile. The only real descriptor that fit was something completely anachronistic. *Dinosaur*.

There were five red-naped ibis on the Semal tree that day. I blinked rapidly, unable to believe it. This was no nimble parakeet turning itself upside down whenever it pleased; no whirring, diaphanous sunbird. I had never seen red-naped ibis (*Pseudibis papillosa*) sitting on a flowering Semal before – it was like seeing meat-eating troglodytes trying to fit in with dainty sunbirds at a vegan festival. The ibis were a collection too, of seemingly odd parts: charcoal-coloured chickens with the legs of a wader and the distant, forbidding demeanour of a predator. Reality needed to stretch itself to make them comprehensible.

What were the ibis doing, I wondered. Because surely, tigers don't eat grass, and ibis will not be interested in flowers. Surely, they were not there for instrumental reasons like feeding, but for reasons of their very own – like wanting to be there. I committed the vision deeply to memory, engraving it into my brain. Three of the birds were unmoving, gargoyle-like in their dignity. One moved its wings and shuffled its position. The fifth one was a juvenile, with a scruffy, pinkish-red carpet for a nape. It dipped its head to inspect the flowers, becoming one with the red petals. It moved about, considering, and then as I watched, it dipped its beak in. The head which would soon grasp and swallow snakes whole took some nectar from the flower.

Could it be? An ibis drinking nectar from a flower on a tree? The sight was completely at odds with the carnivorous diet of the birds I had seen – with hunts procured in areas that were liminal – between mud and water, in the run-down, non-manicured parts of posh parks, but always firmly on the ground. And I realized the tree was not just a roost for a flock, but also a kind of creche for the young one, finding its feet high up in the air.

The Semal had lit my way, showing me a new facet of this dinosaur-bird, and I promised myself I would find a way to swim back to it.

I visited the tree two more times that year. I never saw the ibis feeding on nectar again that year. One bird opened its beak and called – a high, piercing sound. One to wake the sleeping, to chill the hearts of the dead. Or maybe one to tease more Semal buds open. Meanwhile, I was preparing to spend a little more time with the flock. I noticed their stony faces were belied by their expressive calls. Their wings were shiny, almost iridescent, and as the light changed, their form seemed to change too – from fur, to scale, to feather. When they moved, the air seemed to shimmer, as if I were seeing bird-dinosaurs through water. As if the sea of the Covid pandemic were revealing more than detritus.

*

As the Semal flowers fell, and the pandemic raged onwards, the ibis left the tree. And the next spring, April 2021, we got Covid. I was experiencing blackouts, fever, delirium, a loss of the sense of smell. I didn't make things happen; things happened to me. I was meant to keep the promise I had made to myself and solve the ibis-drinking-nectar mystery, but all I was doing was passively holding on to life.

By the time we got back from the hospital, the flowers had fallen. There were no ibis to be seen. A truck horn sounded, loud and unbearable, the new leaves on the Semal shivering at its passage. *You imagined it all*, my mean, Long Covid brain sneered at me. The lockdown sea pulled me underwater, my days lost in brain fog, emerging sometimes for air and comprehension. Around us, the middle class maintained a veneer of haughty survival, not wanting to put out images of despair. My friend's grandmother died gasping and weakened from Covid, but her father wiped the fact from his mind, telling the world she had expired from old age. WhatsApp messages on the virtues of taking steam were forwarded, to compensate for a simmering sense of being diminished by an audacious microbe.

It took me a year to get better. By December 2021, my sense of smell had returned. Slowly, a sense of self was returning, too. The air was cooling. Winter tulips arrowed up from central verges – I saw them twice, walking through the lockdown. Spotted owlets screeched closer, emboldened by the lack of people. In the chill winter air, they emerged as the sun dipped into the horizon. The fog obscured their edges. They were like a dream from childhood: sharp-taloned, unforgettable, but also not fully comprehensible. The awful year was ending, and the fresh air reminded me of brisk March mornings when the Semal would flower again.

By January 2022, I had Covid again. Unlike the Delta variant, this one didn't include a soaring fever. But I had a cough that banged in my chest like a window in a storm. I couldn't sleep at nights despite a bone-deep fatigue that clawed through my days. I wanted to fold myself into a smaller person, embrace my tree-bird memories and perish into something that no longer felt pain.

But spring did come, even if winter seemed never-ending. I craved medicine – the medicine of city trees and wild birds that made do with city trees. The seas of the lockdown were slowly retreating, and my senses were coming back home.

In February 2022, I was standing in front of my lighthouse trees. Finally. I was not dead, and the trees were not dead. I had angled my car forward, parking at the side of a road called Africa Avenue, heart thumping loudly, a little painfully. I looked again at the trees, and they were still there. *Of course they will be here, trees don't move*, my mean Long Covid brain said.

They were there, and they were flowering magnificently, still above it all: the coolness of a god that smiled and smirked in equal measure. So much had changed for me and the world in the last two years. The trees though, were creatures of their own time, and their own realm. They abided like nothing had changed. Perhaps it was this stability we all needed, this calm stoicism that pillared the idea that life did not need to make sense. It just needed to go on.

Today, I could make things happen. I had many things with me: my camera, my eyes, my nose, my lungs that had survived Covid twice over. My yearning for being here strained and stretched from the last two years, the longest span of my life. A span that included time which had complicated and twisted itself right on the tail of my recovery. But today, I'd study the birds until I dropped. I would

IBIS SEA

add to the ibis engravings in my mind.

At first, there were no ibis. The sun climbed higher in the sky, blinding me. Then, slowly, flapping its wings in its curiously unflappable manner, the first ibis came to the tree. Two more followed. Soon, there were five. I wanted to see every movement, hear each call. But this wasn't lockdown anymore. Cars whizzed past, and trucks trundled their way forward. Exhaust fumes hung in the spring air like condensation on an expensive screen you desperately want to keep clean. I kept watching, blocking out other sights and sounds. That's when I heard it: a horrible sound that I had been ignoring since childhood. One that I wouldn't let in, but which gnawed at my consciousness till I had to open the door. It was the sound of a vehicle stopping abruptly, followed by the sound of a man emerging and saying something obscene to me. It doesn't matter what he said, or they said. It has never mattered. There is no substance to the taunts, the jeers, so cutely described as 'eve-teasing' and 'catcalls' by the cops. It is a sound that has chased me, and every girl, in this violent, misogynistic North Indian city. The sound of being unmade as a woman and made into an object and a thing.

One more man stopped his vehicle – a bike this time – and stared at me, his eyes roving over my body like I was a lawn and he would decide how tall the grass would grow. He didn't say anything. He only gazed, like he and his ancestors were entitled to the view. His presence was a spindle at the side of my eye – thicker and colder than the spines on the Semal tree. *Ignore them*, I told myself. *This is my city*, I added as consolation.

But was it? They had ruined my wait for my trees and their otherworldly birds; they had parasitized my rendezvous. The men were all interchangeable in their faces and their intentions, but my specific walk in the woods seemed tainted.

I chanted a list of platitudes to myself, a mantra to stay safe: I was only bending to the wind, and I would not break; I hadn't endured Covid just to bow again, I would return with a friend. Then I got into my red car.

A few days later, my botanist friend Vallari and I were standing at the same spot, looking out with the aspect of pioneers. In my head, I had told myself I would wash the slate clean for that day. Just because I had been harassed each time I was out on the streets didn't mean it would happen again.

The cars whizzed past us, metallic monsters with no conscience. I looked at my friend, dreaming of a kinder city in the whimsical, faintly comic way that close friendships allow. 'I wish all the trees would be Semal. There would be a red skyline in spring then. We should uproot the exotic trees and plant native ones. Also, they should have a longer flowering season...' I said, the words wishful, beads in a necklace I was fingering through. Fumes choked the air – the city's Air Quality Index was climbing back to pre-Covid levels.

She smiled at me through the smoke.

'I almost wish it was the pandemic again. We'd have the place to ourselves,' I carried on.

'No, we don't want that... though it would be better for the wildlife,' she replied, rather kindly.

We watched the trees, waiting for the ibis. In a while, they came. That day, we watched an Indian crow mob the much larger ibis off its perch. Another crow came too, and this one was cawing loudly. If its beak wouldn't work, deafening its subject would. The ibis, bigger and stronger, shifted uneasily, looking uncomfortable with any sort of retaliation. 'This just isn't fair! The crows are generalists, doing much better than the other birds. They just go after every bird they can find,' I cried out. 'At least they can leave the ibis in peace!'

We looked at the scene with hard eyes, wishing for the crows to depart. Cawing and horns filled the air – a soundscape that defines much of city life. Another sound came too. The braking of another car and the disembarking of another man, his jeer shouted at us.

What should we do, my eyes turned to my friend.

'Leave it, we won't confront them,' she said.

In the skyline, the two crows continued mobbing the five ibis on the tree.

*

The next time, we took turns being cops. Our work had transformed from being researchers to becoming bodyguards. It was implicit that only one of us would get her data as the other became the lookout. There were always crows in the sky and men with enough time to stop and harass us. Our relation with our subjects – the ibis and the Semal – was mediated through a series of hiccups, sighs and long swallows. How easily a whistle upended a carefully fought-for sense of self; how simple it was for a shouted taunt to remind one of each time it happened. There were no carefree walks in the woods. There were instead interludes of time snatched by our fierce talons and a deep, dinosaur-like hunger.

We would return at two in the afternoon when we could, when the sun wouldn't be behind the tree or in our eyes. Sometimes the birds weren't there. Sometimes the traffic wouldn't allow us to stand at the side of the road. At all times, people stared, outraged that two women could be doing something other than fetching milk or taking selfies. I don't know if they just wanted to grope us or smash our heads to the ground.

IBIS SEA

We were watching the trees, but not in a private park, shielded by wealth. We were trying to make the trees ours, but we weren't in a wild forest where patriarchy did not enter. We were in a place so commonly occupied that it was called a pedestrian pathway. Only that the privilege to be a pedestrian, to have right of way, to pause, to look around, to loiter, belongs to men. When I told my other friends about the harassment, they frowned. 'Terrible place, that road,' one said.

'Roads are just so bad.' In *sotto voce*: 'All roads.'

'Can't you go when there are no men?'

'But you'll carry on, won't you?' asked another.

I had to carry on, because I had a point to make, and because I had to finish what I had started.[1] 'I wish these trees were in a garden,' Vallari told me one day. We had improvised protecting ourselves from traffic somewhat. Her trusty old car would be parked at the side of the road, an obstruction to eyes from one side, doubling as a platform for cameras. It was our equivalent of a 'hide', only that we were hiding from illegally roving eyes, not from wildlife.

Vallari was looking at the birds through binoculars. I was looking through my camera. 'It's doing it,' she smiled.

Something had happened. The ibis had its head in the flower.

'It's nectaring!' I think we said it together – or that's what it felt like. Our roles of researcher and bodyguard had merged into a single one, a sorority for the Semal. A sisterhood that could, for some moments, enjoy nature with the abandon of a kite soaring uninterrupted in the sky. I snapped photos; she did, too.

In my mind, an idea grew. Could this be the same bird from 2020, all grown up? Would she teach the other ibis to nectar? We used the word 'nectaring' like it was a verb, a private language, a prize – a gob of wild honey in our mouths, washing away the taunts and smoke.

*

Delhi has realized it has a lot of Semal trees, and that means a lot of flowers. The blossoms are the reason the tree was favoured in the city; ironically, they are now leading to the tree's downfall. A profusion of flowers signifies a lot of ground to cover, and clean. Semal flowers create a carpet on the ground with a smooth, slippery consistency. Like a casual, fast fashion change, resident welfare association members have branded the flowers as garbage. The blooms are excessive, and morning walkers say they can slip on them. They find the falling flowers – on the tree for less than two months – so unbearable that they have installed nets under the trees.

Others have asked for head-backing of the trees. In the real forest, the Semal would never be in the minutes of a meeting or a manicuring agenda; but the city is its own kind of tangled forest of egos and outrage.

The generation that valued the city's native trees seems to be less vocal today – people are content to look at foreign frangipanis or feathery palms on the fringes of malls. When the international G20 meeting was held in Delhi, many of the saplings handed out were non-native species. Everyone likes trees, but not everyone likes the Semal, or the *ficus* species like banyans: the trees that spread, that shower the ground with themselves, seeming darkly excessive.

But the bigness of the Semal, its voluptuous flowers, and its sheer force of being have an outlandishness that deserves to survive... Exactly as it is. Because it's ridiculous to expect a tree or a person to tone herself down just because someone says it's too much and too out of place.

For the woman who has been told her lipstick is too red, her voice too loud, even her quiet, circumspect standing at the side of the road too irritating, the Semal is more than florid splendour: it also provides refuge and inspiration.

To stand tall, despite being called garbage. To spread herself far. Find roots of connection with well-meaning men and women, despite facing shouts and smoke. To be so 'too much' that dinosaurs alight on her branches, finding a spot of old-world peace in modern dystopia. To be part of a Nature that has a gentle spirit, even as Nature fights daily battles. A kind of alchemy that thrives in the wild places and survives in the ones right under our noses – avenues, city, sidewalks. The Semal has stoicism and patience, and the ibis has forbearance and its flock community. The Semal grows in both the dustiest and most germane of places; the ibis has an appreciation for a quick hunt and gentle honeyed sip both. They seem to know their strengths thoroughly – and they have upturned all the bookish learning I had of them. In seeing the ibis take nectar from a native tree, I have learnt it is not people but the birds themselves that are my teachers.

I have nothing to prove this, but I sense both tree and bird have a spirit that is tougher and gentler than the worst ideas of people and society. On some days, I want to have the Semal's deep-rooted sure-footedness; on other days I want the hunger of the ibis. Both are sources of power that are untainted by society's insecurities: strong, but not easily baited, living quietly amidst us, waiting to be noticed by those who need them. My anger – at my places being barred by men – laps against the trunks of the trees. It eddies, inspecting the pillar. It watches the tree and the combinations it offers – ibis-Semal,

IBIS SEA

ibis-smoke, crow-ibis – and the pain changes a bit, becoming less plump.

I think the tree shows me how to alchemize my feelings; make them something more or less; but different from how they started out. It teaches me to extract something good from the rotten, how to use lighthouses to turn my submergence into buoyancy. It transforms a diseased sea into my own ibis-sea. It teaches me, perhaps, how to take violence and make it power.

And I think then: me, and women like me, will get through.

One tree at a time.

One ibis at a time.

ENDNOTES

HOPE IS THE THING WITH FLIPPERS

1. All details of the whale's life and death are from Richard Sabin and Lorraine Cornish, *Hope*, Natural History Museum, 2019.

2. 'a symbol of hope for the future of the natural world.' is a quote from NHM Director Michael Dixon in ibid.

3. All name and word origins are from the OED.

4. US Supreme Court judgement, available at: https://www.supremecourt.gov/opinions/23pdf/23-124_8nk0.pdf

5. 'Greta Thunberg: Our House Is On Fire! | World Economic Forum 2019' - youtube.com, also Greta Thunberg, *No one is too small to make a difference*, 2019.

6. Aldo Leopold, A Sand County Almanac, 1949.

7. Caroline Hickman et al, 'Climate anxiety in children and young people and their beliefs about government responses to climate change: a global survey.' *The Lancet* Planetary Health 5, e863–e873 (2021).

8. Dan Bortolotti, *Wild Blue*, 2008.

9. Philip Hoare, Leviathan or, The Whale, 2009.

10. Bortolotti, ibid.

11. Sabin and Cornish, ibid.

12. Charlotte Epstein, *The Power of Language in International Relations'*, 2008. Whaling in the 20th century; D. Graham Burnett, The Sounding of the Whale, 2013; Hoare, ibid.

13. Hoare, ibid.

ENDNOTES

14. Arthur Conan Doyle, 'Life on a Greenland Whaler', Strand Magazine, Jan 1897.

15. 'Davis' Straits Fishing'. *The Aberdeen Journal*. No. 4318. 13 October 1830.

16. Tom Mole, *The Secret Life of Books*, 2020.

17. Subhadra Das and Miranda Lowe. (2018). Nature Read in Black and White: decolonial approaches to interpreting natural history collections. Journal of Natural Science Collections, 2018. [online] 6, pp.4–14. Available at: http://www.natsca.org/article/2509

18. Richard Owen, *On the Extent and Aims of a National Museum of Natural History*, 1862. Available at: https://archive.org/details/b21954318/page/n9/mode/2up [Accessed 22 Apr. 2023].

19. Maciej Wójtowicz, 'Repatriation of human remains' whatdotheyknow.com, December 2018, Available at: www.whatdotheyknow.com/request/repatriation_of_human_remains_2?utm_campaign=alaveteli-experiments-87&utm_content=sidebar_similar_requests&utm_medium=link&utm_source=whatdotheyknow. [Accessed 22 Apr. 2023].

20. John Holmes, 'Pre-Raphaelite architecture and scientific controversy after Darwin: the natural history museum versus nature'. In: *The Pre Raphaelites and Science*. 2018.

21. Graham Readfearn, Leo Hickman and Rupert Neate, 'Michael Hintze revealed as funder of Lord Lawson's climate thinktank', March 2012. <https://www.theguardian.com/environment/2012/mar/27/tory-donor-climate-sceptic-thinktank> [Accessed 22 Apr. 2023].

22. Helena Horton, 'Climate sceptic thinktank reported to charity commission over fossil fuel interest funding', 2022. Available at: https://amp.theguardian.com/environment/2022/may/23/fossil-fuel-funded-think-tank-charity-commission-global-warming. [Accessed 22

ENDNOTES

Apr. 2023].

23. Nicola Pearson, 'Central Hall renamed following £5m gift', May 2014. Available at: https://www.nhm.ac.uk/discover/news/2014/may/central-hall-renamed-following-five-million-gift.html [Accessed 22 Apr. 2023].

24. Matthew Cockram, 'Geological Society, Hintze and Fossil Fuel Connections', July 2023. Available at: https://www.whatdotheyknow.com/request/geological_society_hintze_and_fo#incoming-2395809 [Accessed 22 Apr. 2023].

25. For all descriptions of the Petroleum Group's Awards Dinners, I'm grateful to have interviewed a petroleum geologist present at many of these events, and who has asked not to be named.

26. 'Grand Ball Given by the Whales.' Drawing. *Vanity Fair.* April 20, 1861.

27. Hoare, ibid.

28. Paul Watson, *The War that Saved the Whales: The Confederate War Against the Yankee Whalers.* 2019.

29. Richard York, 'Why Petroleum Did Not Save the Whales', 2017. Socius, 3. https://doi.org/10.1177/2378023117739217

30. Rogers, N. (2019). The Geological Society of London - Getting involved. [online] www.geolsoc.org.uk. Available at: https://www.geolsoc.org.uk/Geoscientist/Archive/June-2020/People-News [Accessed 22 Apr. 2023].

31. Extinction Rebellion . *Extinction Rebellion Dinner of HOPE at the NHM.* [online] www.facebook.com. 2019. Available at: https://www.facebook.com/events/843489362677427/?active_tab=about [Accessed 22 Apr. 2023].

32. Ibid.

33. Real Media. *A Night at the Natural History Museum.*

ENDNOTES

[online] www.youtube.com. 2019. Available at: https://www.youtube.com/watch?v=PaqcZzUFubs&embeds_euri=https%3A%2F%2Frealmedia.press%2F&source_ve_path=MjM4NTE&feature=emb_title [Accessed 22 Apr. 2023].

34. Extinction Rebellion. 18 June: *Extinction Rebellion meet with Natural History Museum ahead of action.* [online] Extinction Rebellion UK. 2019. Available at: https://extinctionrebellion.uk/2019/06/18/18-june-extinction-rebellion-meet-with-natural-history-museum-ahead-of-action/ [Accessed 22 Apr. 2023].

35. Emily Dickinson, 'Hope is the Thing with Feathers'. Fascicle 13, c. 1861.

36. Greta Thunberg. *The Climate Book*. 2022.

37. 'Natural History Museum declares "Planetary Emergency" and reveals bold new Vision and Strategy to 2031 in response', 2022. Available at: https://www.nhm.ac.uk/press-office/press-releases/natural-history-museum-declares--planetary-emergency--and-reveal.html [Accessed 22 Apr. 2023].

38. Geological Society, 'Energy Group, 2020. Available at: https://www.geolsoc.org.uk/energygroup#:~:text=%EE%80%80The%20Energy%20Group%20of [Accessed 22 Apr. 2023].

39. Rebecca Solnit, *Hope in the Dark*, 2016.

40. Natural History Museum 'Dippy about the whale with Lorraine Cornish and Richard Sabin | #NHM_Live', May 2017. Available at: https://www.youtube.com/watch?v=B3YeXqgF8lc [Accessed 22 Apr. 2023].

ENDNOTES

IBIS SEA

1. i The findings of this study offered novel perspectives on red-naped ibis taking nectar from *Bombax ceiba* flowers. The study, 'Nectar in the diet of the red-naped Ibis' was published in the journal *Stork, Ibis and Spoonbill Conservation* in 2022.

THE JUDGES

DAVID COOPER is a Senior Lecturer in the Department of English at Manchester Metropolitan University where he is the Founding Co-Director of the Centre for Place Writing. He co-edited *The Routledge Handbook of Literary Geographies* (2024) and is writing on the immersiveness of contemporary place writing for Liverpool University Press. Other creative-critical publications include the pamphlet *The Duddon Estuary: The Myriad Lines of its Relations* (2022), and an essay, 'The Most Mancunian of Trees', in Saraband's *North Country* anthology (2022) edited by Karen Lloyd.

MARCHELLE FARRELL is a writer, medical psychotherapist, and amateur gardener. Born in Trinidad and Tobago, she has spent more than twenty years attempting to become hardy in the UK. She is curious about the relationship between our external and internal landscapes, the patterns we re-enact in relation to the land, and how they might be changed. When not caring for her children, or working in the community, Marchelle is in her Somerset garden, or writing on what it teaches her about herself. Her debut book, *Uprooting* (2023), won the Nan Shepherd Prize 2021 and was shortlisted for the Wainwright Prize 2024.

THE JUDGES

KIM KREMER is MD of Notting Hill Editions, an independent publisher specialising in literary essays with over sixty collections to its name. Publications include *Embrace Fearlessly the Burning World*, by the late nature writer Barry Lopez. In 2013, Notting Hill Editions launched its Essay Prize, which Kim continued to run until 2017. After starting her publishing career in London, Kim pursued an interest in environmental issues and spent two years working at the Centre for Alternative Technology, an eco-centre in Powys, Wales, dedicated to demonstrating and teaching sustainable development.

JAMIE NORMINGTON works to inspire others about nature and taking action for wildlife as Cumbria Wildlife Trust's Learning and Development Manager. In 2019, he embarked on a 200-mile coast-to-coast walk, with Robert Macfarlane and Jackie Morris's book *The Lost Words*, and called in at primary schools and community centres to speak about the ideas in the book. He has written columns for regional papers ranging from Poland's *Trybuna Opolska* to the Brighton Argus; appeared on BBC radio and television; and most recently contributed to the BTO's *Into the Red* book on endangered wildlife.

OWEN SHEERS (Chair) is a multi-award-winning author, poet and playwright. He is Professor in Creativity at Swansea University and Ambassador

THE JUDGES

and co-founder of Black Mountains College, an HE organisation for sustainable futures. His 2023 film *Cynefin* highlighted the new ecologically focused management plan for the Bannau Brycheiniog national park and reclaimed 'an old name for a new way of being'. His writings include poetry collections, novels, verse dramas and multiple works for TV, film and theatre. Collaborative projects include a BBC drama, *The Trick*, about the 2009 Climategate affair and an environmental opera with Welsh National Opera. In 2004 he was Writer in Residence at The Wordsworth Trust.

ACKNOWLEDGEMENTS

Principally, the Nature Chronicles Prize would like to thank all those who entered our competition. We are as awestruck by your talent as last time – perhaps even more so. Several surprising and illuminating books could have been created out of your original, contemporary insights. Our thanks also to our readers – we have a great team – and our judges: what a weekend that was.

This prize, we were honoured to partner with Booths supermarket – thank you so much both from us and from those entrants you sponsored. Also deserving of recognition for their support are Gail Knopfel and Lakeland Arts, Paul Scully and Kendal Mountain Book Festival, and Honor and Madeleine Scott.

Finally, thanks to Sara Hunt at Saraband books: queen.

PRUDENCE MARY SCOTT, née Milligan, was born in 1926 to a naval family. She was given a Quaker education and then trained as a nurse. In 1952 she married and in 1961 moved to the Lake District, where she brought up her four children, mostly as a single parent. It was a quiet, contained sort of existence, which immersed her children in nature: hedgehogs, Fell ponies, curlews. She was a great reader, and sometimes painted and sometimes wrote poetry – but always she kept up with her journals. In them, she observes her children and her surroundings with the same restless, curious, unsentimental eye.

She died in London on 1 September 2019, aged ninety-three.